Pharmacy Marketing Formulary

Marketing for pharmacy people

To Deborah,

Thanks,

Gavin.

Gavin Birchall
BPharm Hons, FRPharmS, PGCert Management, MA Graphic Design

Notice

First Edition 2018

Published by DOSE Publishing Limited, a company registered in England and Wales with company number 10219192 and whose registered office is at 2 Newton Road, Ashton-on-Ribble, Preston, Lancashire, PR2 1DY.

For further information on DOSE Publishing Limited's products and services, please visit www.dosepublishing.uk.

Computerset by DOSE Publishing Limited.

Printed and bound by Ingram Spark, Milton Keynes, United Kingdom.

ISBN: 978 1 9164042 0 5.

Contents

Context   6

Strategic considerations   28

    Step one | Orientation and research   30

    Step two | Segmentation, targeting and positioning   52

    Step three | Goals   94

Tactical choices   108

    Step four | Product, price, place and promotion   110

    Step five | People, physical evidence and process   160

Brand   190

References   202

Glossary   204

The author   206

Call to action   208

Context

From the moment we wake to the moment we sleep we are bombarded with messages from people who want to sell us something. These messages are the end result of the *marketing* process. They are the culmination of a lot of research, analysis and thought that defines exactly what the message is trying to get across, where, when and to whom.

At least they should be if the people creating the messages understand marketing and have put the effort into developing and implementing a robust marketing *strategy*. The large multiple pharmacy chains and the independent networks have a team of marketers at their disposal. Many medium sized chains also have a marketing function of some sort. As an employed pharmacist you need to be aware of what your marketing team is up to, so that you can amplify the effect rather than accidentally suppress it.

If you own a pharmacy or aspire to own a pharmacy then you need to understand how to create and implement a good marketing strategy yourself, so that you can compete with and beat your competition, protect and grow your market share and develop new products that will benefit both your patients and your business.

Everyone working in pharmacy needs to understand how to harness the power of the marketing process to succeed against potential external competitors and secure the future of the profession.

The 5 steps and 64 ideas in this book will help you do that.

The value of marketing

Marketing above all business functions is often misunderstood. That is not a surprise. Unlike other functions that deal with fixed quantities that can be repeatedly manipulated with a known outcome, marketing deals with humans who constantly change and resist all attempts at pinning them down. As people change and the world around them changes, so your marketing has to develop to keep up. It is a mixture of science and creativity which often frightens a lot of business people, because it is difficult to quantify.

However, if you are interested in what your customers feel, think and do, then you cannot underestimate the value of marketing.

It shouldn't be a mystery. Good marketing strategy, our focus, is based on a process informed by evidence. That process is what I aim to arm you with.

I am a pharmacist who has successfully established, grown and managed community pharmacies across the country. I was Superintendent Pharmacist, Operations and Marketing Director for an innovative group of 20 pharmacies that consistently outperformed the market. Early on during that period I was aware of an idea that I couldn't quite reach. Something I felt but couldn't articulate. A really important something. Possibly the key something that defines whether a pharmacy is successful or not. So I looked for language that helped me give shape to that idea. I found marketing. It was a revelation. I set up a pharmacy specialist design and marketing agency to help pharmacists harness these ideas.

As with any worthwhile subject there are differing opinions about what is right and what is wrong. The ideas in this book represent a robust, evidence based, step by step way of developing and implementing a marketing strategy to help you achieve your business goals. They work for me and they work for my clients.

If you get your marketing right you will make more money. More customers will be aware of how your products meet their needs and they will be more likely to purchase from you.

Marketing means more.

If you get your marketing wrong you will not be making as much money as you could for the opposite reasons. It is a sliding scale and even if you are doing some things well there are always ways to improve.

Marketing means more.

As you will come to appreciate, marketing is the interface between your pharmacy and your customers. It is how you shape the experience they have of your pharmacy. It is the only way to do it with any real deliberate intent. It is how you inform and update their view of what you can offer them and how it will help them. Those experiences will determine whether your customers choose to use your pharmacy or another one.

That is the only decision that matters.

It's a pretty important one.

'Those who stop marketing to save money are like those who stop a clock to save time.'

Henry Ford | Founder of Ford Motor Company

What is marketing?

When supplying a prescription only medicine to a patient, they only see the last step in a complex process. You check their identity, provide relevant counselling and give them their medicines. This short interaction relies on a huge amount of work being completed beforehand.

Good marketing is the same. The actual contact with the customer is a short interaction at the end of a complex process and a lot of work. It involves really understanding how you can help a specific person with something they need and how to make money while you are at it.

Then and only then should you think about telling them about it. You won't win their attention often, so get it right from the start by thinking before you act.

The most successful companies develop the best understanding of their customers and then execute spectacularly well.

You may wonder where branding fits into the equation. Your pharmacy brand is the result of the marketing process. It is the thoughts and feelings that your customers have about your pharmacy, which are a cumulative result of the experiences they have whenever they come into contact with it. Marketing is how you influence those thoughts and feelings. We will return to branding as we approach the end of the marketing process.

'Marketing is the science
and art of exploring, creating
and delivering value to satisfy
the needs of a target market
at a profit.'

Dr. Philip Kotler, Professor of International Marketing,
Kellogg School of Management, Northwestern University

Marketing definitions

You can find definitions of many important terms (in italic the first time they appear in the main text) in the glossary. The marketing definition is not always the same as the common definition so it is worthwhile taking a look.

For example a product in marketing terms is 'anything that can be offered to a market for attention, acquisition, use or consumption' (Kotler, P) and whenever I use the word product, that is my meaning. It includes physical products and services, even ideas.

A customer is a person who invests in a product. Their time, energy, belief or money. For your pharmacy this includes not just patients and shoppers but commissioners, fellow healthcare professionals, local politicians and so on. You can use the ideas in this book to help you influence stakeholders in all directions.

'Marketing is not only much broader than selling. It is not a specialised activity at all. It is the whole business seen from the point of view of the final result, that is, from the customer's point of view.'

Peter Drucker, Management Consultant, Educator, Author

Everything you do is marketing

The marketing process culminates with a communication that carries a message and compels the customer to take action. Everything a person senses when they come into contact with your pharmacy, whether physically, on the phone, online or via a delivery, communicates something and adds to their overall view of your business.

Your customers won't separate what you consider to be your marketing efforts from your operations, your logistics or any other part of your business. They decide whether to use your pharmacy based on the total sum of what they experience, whether you want them to or not.

Make sure they experience something good.

Everything you do sends a message.

Everything you do is marketing.

Market deliberately, not accidentally

You wouldn't accidentally manage your financial accounts, or accidentally complete your CD register, so make sure that you take action and avoid accidental marketing. A failure to deliberately take control of your marketing with the aim of influencing your customer's experience does not mean that their decisions about where to source pharmaceutical care won't be affected by that experience. It just means that you have no idea how it will be affected and that you are not managing it. It could be a positive influence but it is more likely that it will be neutral or negative.

Don't leave it to chance.

Think about what you want to communicate to your customers, then list every point at which your pharmacy comes into contact with them, known as *touch points*. A sequential list of touch points from beginning to end is sometimes called the customer journey. Map it out. For each individual product if you are really determined. Ask your customers how satisfied they are with their experience at each of those points and how you could make it better. Then work through the process of improving every touch point as much as possible. The combined effect will give people reasons to use your pharmacy and not your competition.

Market deliberately, not accidentally.

Marketing is not technology

New technology changes things. Mass manufacturing was the beginning of the end for extemporaneous dispensing in the 1960s. Personal computing made everyone a publisher in the 1980s. Smart phones have now made us all citizen journalists. New technology is changing marketing too. It's exciting and often promises the world.

The huge growth in the number and type of digital communication channels in recent years has distracted many in marketing and caused them to focus on the way they are communicating rather than what they are communicating. Both are important but the 'what' has to come first. Communicate the wrong message to the wrong people in a thousand new ways and it won't help you sell any more of your product.

Take the average tablet. It has been carefully formulated to deliver the active ingredient. It is a vector. A delivery method. It is the same with communication channels. They are the vector. The delivery method. They are not the active ingredient. The marketing message is the active ingredient. Don't get distracted by the vector before you perfect your active ingredient.

Technology will change and how you communicate with your customers will change with it. Technology is a tool with which to do a job. You can't know which tool will work best until you know what the job is. Your marketing strategy defines the job.

Overcome the marketing challenge

Think about how much time you spend working out the best way to deliver a pharmacy service. Processes, procedures and such. Think about how much time you spend working out how to make money while doing that. Financial models, targets, forecasting and purchasing. Now think about how much time you spend working out if what you are delivering is what the customer actually wants, if it meets their needs and how to make sure they are satisfied at the end of it all!

Many of you will spend the vast majority of time thinking about the first two and that is to be expected. Most people do. Pharmacy is a very complex profession and much thought is needed to make sure that you are operating safely, legally, efficiently and profitably.

The demands of the day to day can dominate our time. The prescriptive nature of our NHS contract and the profitability of pharmacy in decades past has blinkered us into this mindset. There was plenty to go around so we focused on delivering what came through the door as profitably as possible. This is the operational challenge. We are excellent at it. Too good in fact. So good that we have made it look easy and now that times have changed and funding through NHS contracts is dwindling we find ourselves caught out. The end result is a set of misconceptions held by many healthcare commissioners and politicians about our contribution, that we are struggling to overturn.

We need to relearn what we once knew. Reawaken our entrepreneurial spirit and sharpen our skills. We need new income from new sources and to do that we need to think about customers who aren't the NHS i.e. individuals or organisations. We need to understand what they want and how we can meet their needs better than our competitors. This is the marketing challenge. It comes before the operational challenge and is arguably more important. If you understand and implement the ideas in this book you will understand how to overcome the marketing challenge, regain your entrepreneurial drive and work on how to secure the future of your pharmacy.

How to succeed

You are an intelligent person. You recognise areas where you need to improve your knowledge and skill and you are ready to do something about it. We know you are inquisitive and committed. Success in marketing will rely on both of these qualities and a range of others.

Vision

You will need to have an idea of what it is you want to market before you start. This might be your existing pharmacy, a new pharmacy, existing products or new products. In any case, try and capture in writing what it is that you aspire to achieve with your endeavour. Some people call this a vision or a mission statement. It doesn't matter what you call it but defining it does matter. Keep it short. Keep it aspirational. Keep it easy to understand. Keep it in mind while developing your marketing strategy.

Focus

Marketing is full of marketers. They like to use the same ideas we will explore to convince you to invest in their methodologies or products. It is easy to get lost in marketing unless you are careful. Follow the process outlined in this book and you will benefit from a clear, robust approach after which you can explore additional methods.

Determination

Learning and applying anything new can seem tough. I have aimed to make this book easy to read and I've crammed a lot of ideas into a small number of pages. This is not a text book. It is intended to inspire. Quickly. Get to the end of this book. Scribble in the margins as you go. Write notes. Go back through it again. Implement some of the ideas. Test them. Adjust your approach.

You will also need to carry out research, planning, objective setting, writing, financial analysis, apply your creativity and document your work to a professional standard at each step of the process.

'Marketing strategy is where we play and how we win in the market. Tactics are how we then deliver on the strategy and execute for success.'

Mark Ritson, Adjunct Professor of Marketing, Melbourne Business School

Strategy then *tactics*

Think before you act. A simple concept but one that is easy to lose site of in the cut and thrust of running a busy pharmacy. A skill gap within marketing has arisen around strategy development in recent years. This coincides closely with the expansion in the number of communication channels available and the almost limitless options they offer. Far too much focus on tactics and far too little on strategy. People are fixating on the communication channel and what it can do rather than the message and what it communicates. The vector rather than the active ingredient. Both matter but the active ingredient comes first.

Communicating without thinking about what you are communicating, to whom and why is a waste of time and money. Resist the temptation to jump straight in and start communicating with customers just because it's easy. Some of your competitors may be doing this which is great. When you have worked out what you want to say in a way that will compel your customers to use your pharmacy, your communications will be much more effective and you can win market share.

Strategy then tactics. Strategy then tactics. Strategy then tactics.

Say it out loud.

The marketing process

Hopefully you will have picked up by now where we are going to begin. That's right, strategy. The marketing process can be broken down into two, major, sequential parts. Say it again. Strategy then tactics.

Strategic considerations

Strategic considerations include orientation, research, segmentation, targeting and *positioning*. We will look at these as three steps. The first step is diagnostic, the second prescriptive and the third objective. Once you have been through these steps you should have a good idea of who will be likely to buy your products, who the most attractive customers are and why and how to present your pharmacy or product to appeal to them.

You'll review how your pharmacy is currently operating, do some research into what your customers actually think and (even more importantly) how they behave, choose which groups of customers to spend your marketing budget communicating with and make some key decisions about what you want to stand for in your customers' minds.

Tactical choices

Tactical choices include how you will design, price, distribute, promote and deliver your product. These again split into two steps. Steps four, product design and step five, product delivery.

The aim is to find the combination of choices that has the highest possible appeal to your target customers while delivering an acceptable and sustainable level of profit for your pharmacy.

Each of the five steps builds on the last and uses information and decisions made earlier on. If you stick to the process without missing out any of the key parts you will end up with a useful strategy that makes sense, that you can implement and monitor and that will have an impact.

Real world application

At the end of each step I've described in a case study how you might apply the marketing process in your pharmacy, specifically to a stop smoking service. Smoking is the most significant lifestyle risk factor and the vast majority of pharmacists have come across this kind of service. You might have experience of setting up a stop smoking service or delivering one in practice, which can act as a point of reference and comparison. Remember that the case study is just an example. The data, actions and outcomes are illustrative. It is deliberately not exhaustive. There is room for you to consider how you might add to or adapt the approach taken.

Keeping it simple

To help you put all of the pieces together I have designed a model that looks at each important aspect of developing your strategy and making tactical choices in turn. You will meet the model on the next two pages and then at the beginning of each key part of the marketing process to help you orientate yourself and keep track of where you are up to.

Fig 1. The drop marketing model: From idea to communication

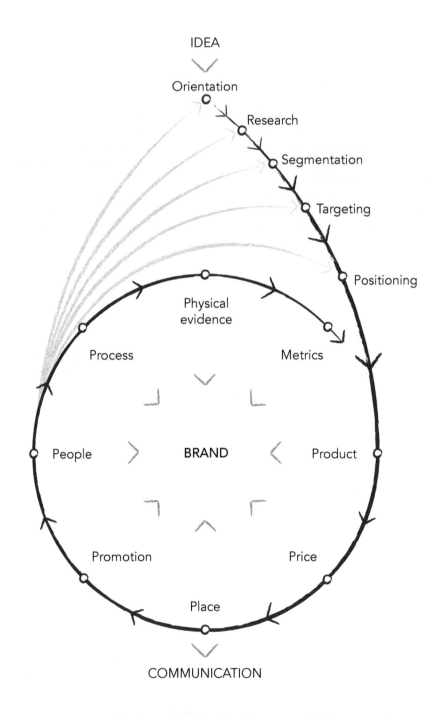

The drop marketing model

The drop was once a common dosage unit and as you know is still used for eye and nasal drops. This humble unit inspired the design of the drop marketing model.

From idea to communication

The model starts with an idea. This may be your pharmacy business or a new product. The idea is then taken through the different stages of the marketing process and results in carefully considered, confident communications.

Beginning with the strategic considerations we work through Step one, Orientation and Research and move onto Step two, Segmentation, Targeting and Positioning. These considerations form a strategic arc, preceding and informing tactical choices.

From there we move onto the tactical choices themselves covering the remaining steps in the process which highlight the cyclical, interconnected nature of marketing tactics.

The combination of choices results in your customers' experience of your pharmacy i.e. your brand.

You may at times decide that no matter how you adjust your tactics you just aren't getting the results you want or expect. That is the time to break out of the tactical cycle and return to the strategic arc. Even good tactics can't fix bad strategy.

This is our model.

We will be looking at each step in detail, always in context, and building your understanding of marketing.

Apply as required

The marketing process we are about to explore can be applied at a number of different levels to your pharmacy business and the products that you offer. Indeed it could be applied to the pharmacy profession as a whole. The detail will differ depending on what you are aiming to achieve but the process will always be broadly the same.

Business level

You may consider developing a marketing strategy for your pharmacy as a whole to help you understand how best to achieve your long term goals, to appeal to your customers and to successfully compete. This is a great place to start and will help you to raise awareness and appear distinct.

Category level

You may consider developing a marketing strategy for a group of products that help with a particular kind of need. Nutrition for example. This is a good second step for your more important products to help raise awareness, educate customers and ultimately drive sales.

Product level

You may consider developing a marketing strategy for an individual product to raise awareness and maximise sales. Remember the marketing definition of a product includes services.

So many decisions that might have you stumped or paralysed at the moment will become obvious when you have a strategy in place. It is almost miraculous and feels great to know what to do next and to understand why you are doing it. When you have implemented your strategy the results will guide its continued development and you really start learning what works for your business, your customers and your market. You will get better and better.

You may have read about or even worked on social media strategies, content strategies etc, which are all fine but they are a part of an overall marketing strategy. They are really about how to use the communications channels and focus on optimising tactics rather than a marketing strategy itself. Don't get the two confused.

After developing your marketing strategy you will do well to review your touch points and enhance them in whatever ways are necessary. A new visual identity perhaps. Certainly refreshing your verbal identity. New signage. Website redevelopment. Social media review and activity. Be thorough. When your touch points are consistent, coherent and get across what you want to stand for you can move onto delivering integrated marketing campaigns that communicate key messages about your products, activities and so on.

Just hang on there a minute though. Looking at touch points or campaigns would be jumping ahead to implementation. We are interested in strategy not implementation here, so lets focus on each of the strategic considerations in turn to start with.

Strategic intent

For a long time we in the pharmacy profession have not had to think broadly about what we offer society and perhaps we have forgotten how to do so. The NHS contract has provided and we have, if we are being blunt, taken that for granted. The world has turned and we now need to re-learn or at least re-consider our activity in the widest context to take hold of our future and secure it in spite of external challenges. This is the strategic arc. The pharmacy profession as we know it began over 100 years before the NHS was created and it prospered before and since 1948. It can continue to prosper when we remember our past and define our future. To do that we need to collectively act with strategic intent.

Strategic considerations

Strategy is the work that helps us answer some big questions.

+ What is my goal?
+ Who are my customers?
+ What do they need?
+ How can I satisfy those needs?
+ What do I want to stand for in their minds?
+ How can I make best use of my resources?

There are three steps. They will help you answer some of those questions in more detail and to inform your tactical choices later in the marketing process.

+ Step one | Diagnostic
+ Step two | Prescriptive
+ Step three | Objective

Step one

Step one looks at diagnosing your current marketing condition, realigning your orientation towards the customer and gathering data about how best to satisfy them.

Diagnostic

+ Orientation
+ Research

IDEA

[Orientation]

Researc

Se

Orientation

Orientation looks at what you consider most important.

'A satisfied customer is the best business strategy of all.'

Michael LeBoeuf, Former Professor of Management, University of New Orleans

You are a customer but you are not your customer

You are deeply engrossed in running your pharmacy. You've been doing it for years. You eat, sleep and breathe it because that is what it takes to make it work. You might be tempted to think that this means you intuitively know what your customers want.

Resist this temptation with all of your might. When you are part of production you cease to be a consumer and no matter how hard you try, you won't be able to effectively put yourself in your customers' shoes. It is critical to recognise this. Know in your heart, that your opinion is not just irrelevant, it might be dangerous because you are biased.

Your primary goal is customer satisfaction. Without it you can't achieve any of your other goals. You must build your business around it. Some people call this customer focus, others customer orientation. We'll call it market orientation. Having the humility to accept that you can't know what your customer wants is the personal challenge of market orientation. If you can do this you will have taken the most important step towards marketing your business because it leaves you in the dark and drives you to find answers. You find answers by connecting with your customers and listening. These answers are your marketing strategy.

It isn't enough for you to adopt a market orientation, your entire team need to do so too. Your organisation needs to be structured to focus on understanding and delivering what your customers want. This is the organisational challenge of market orientation. As a leader in your organisation it is up to you to set this direction for others to follow.

Point in the direction of your customers.

Always.

Don't just say it, actually do it

Almost everyone will tell you they are focussed on satisfying customers. Far fewer actually do so. They might mean to but there are many barriers in the way that make it difficult.

Cost of implementation, fear of change, time taken to adjust, reliance on assumptions rather than evidence and the belief that you actually do know it all, are key barriers that make adopting a market orientation hard. It's a real challenge for both the individual and the organisation. Accept that you don't know everything, seek evidence and know that it will cost more in both time and money in the long run to adopt any other orientation.

If you sell whatever you produce just because you always have, then you have a product orientation and might think that marketing is education. If you are only concerned with sales, then you have a sales orientation and will think that marketing is sales. If you are only interested in what customers can see, then you have an advertising orientation and probably think marketing is communications.

In a large organisation, specialist departments may need different orientations but the organisation as a whole, the senior team and the marketing team need a marketing orientation. If you are a pharmacy owner operator you need to think like a marketer and be the customer champion. Don't fight against your team. Take them with you and lead by instruction and example.

Be humble, let your opinion go

If you are to adopt a market orientation and start building customer satisfaction into everything that you do, you are going to need to be humble and let your personal opinions go.

It's hard. Really hard. Market orientation places customers' opinions above your own.

It can be even harder for pharmacists because we almost always know more about the products we offer to meet a clinical need than our customers. Part of our role is to define the clinical need in the first place. We are healthcare professionals not shopkeepers. The knowledge balance is different.

Confusion arises when a particular customer sees things differently. We work in a retail environment so they might expect their relationship with us to be similar to those they have with retailers. We can't blame them really.

However, meeting a customer's clinical need does not always result in their satisfaction. They have their own set of needs that are separate to their clincial need and only sometimes overlap. We could call those customer needs. Our job is to satisfy both the clincial and customer needs.

Customers will always know more about what will satisfy them than we do. The puzzle is trying to understand what that is and matching our knowledge, skills and resources to achieving it.

Accept that and realise that your success hinges on understanding customer needs in as much depth as you can. Commit yourself to it. Dedicate yourself to it. As an action not just an ideal.

Orientation actions

1. Accept that as the producer you do not know what your customers want.

2. Review how your pharmacy operates through the lens of market orientation. Identify and list aspects of the operation that have an alternative orientation (product, sales, advertising etc) and put a plan in place to adjust that orientation.

3. Plan a workshop session with your team to share the idea of market orientation, ask for input about changes that will help you to adopt a market orientation as a team. Implement. Monitor. Follow up.

Orientation notes

Research

Research looks at strengthening the information you use to make decisions.

Replace beliefs with knowledge

Fill the knowledge gap left by accepting a market orientation with real evidence gathered through market research. Actually communicate with your customers. Not just responsively when you are serving them. Pro-actively ask them how you can do better.

In reality you are learning about how best to satisfy your customers' needs all of the time. Every day. They tell you in many little ways. Implicitly. The longer you've been practising the more you will have picked up and the more convincing your experiences will feel in terms of guiding your beliefs. Your beliefs will guide your behaviour. Far better to base your behaviour on explicit information that you have gathered directly from your customers rather than your perception of their implicit feedback.

It is uncommon to make business decisions based on beliefs. We tend to want something a little more substantial than that. Something a little more reliable. The consequences of making the wrong decision are significant. Especially when we are dealing with people's health. When supplying a medicine and counselling a patient about potential interactions we would rely on scientific evidence to support us. Understanding how to satisfy your customers should be no different.

Replace your beliefs with knowledge learnt through well executed market research and you can start to make decisions more confidently.

Start with what you want to know

Begin your research by defining as closely as possible what you don't know, the kind of answers that you want, the kind of questions that will get them and the people you will need to ask. You will have a much higher chance of learning what you need to know.

It may sound obvious but starting with the gaps in your knowledge makes a lot of sense. Why ask about what you already know? How do you know what you don't know you might ask? It's not that paradoxical. You have an idea in your mind for a product that you think will satisfy your customers. You'll want to know whether your instinct is right and to what extent. Begin with wide open questions to determine the big picture and narrow them down to uncover more specific details. Unless there is a clear target market e.g. patients with a specific condition, you'll want to ask as diverse a group as possible. Ask about your group's personal details, their attitudes and beliefs and their behaviours.

Tailor your process to your enquiry. That is, you would approach finding out whether people like the new delivery van design differently to finding out why your prescription numbers are consistently down. Both are market research but they will need differing methods to uncover the truth. As you progress through the different stages of research you will need to keep asking yourself what questions you want answering next.

Secondary first

You can learn a lot by gathering and analysing information that is already freely available at no cost but your time.

Secondary research, that is using information that others have captured and shared, is the easiest and often the most instantly rewarding type of research. It is the process of finding pre-existing data that is usually free and immediately available. Start your market research there using web search, social media, prior research and third party reports. You will often get a close to accurate estimate of what you are looking for, so this is a great way to carry out initial scoping of a new product idea.

As a bare minimum when operating a pharmacy, you should keep up to date with the key documents outlining the priorities and strategies of NHS and Government bodies responsible for public health in your area. You can dive into more detail to investigate specific opportunities when necessary.

There are some obvious flaws with secondary research and you must be cautious and use your common sense. You rarely get exactly the right data, it can often be outdated, the sample may be unrepresentative and you must assess the credibility of each information source. Investigate and satisfy yourself of the validity and value of a source before you rely on it during your decision making.

The issues that matter

Often you will need more than existing information to answer your key questions. You will need to carry out primary research, that is capturing entirely new information. There are two main areas of primary research. *Qualitative* and *quantitative*. Each have their merits and they are strongest when used together. Start with qualitative to understand the market, then move to quantitative to measure the market.

You can't quantify what you can't name and describe. Begin with qualitative research and aim to understand the kind of issues that matter to your customers. If you don't, you risk finding out a lot of detail about the wrong things. What matters to a young parent compared to an elderly person living alone may be very different. Both may need prescription collection and delivery but for different reasons. This information could help you develop your product to better satisfy each groups' needs.

There are a range of ways to conduct qualitative research but to keep it simple consider holding a *focus group* or two and listen to your customers. Another method is to watch your customers when they are using your product.

How much do they matter?

When you have learnt about the issues that matter to your customers, the next step is understanding how much they matter and to how many. Ask the right questions and provide a sensible scale for responses and you will have some useful numerical data to drive the decisions you make when developing your marketing strategy.

The number of people who you can involve in a focus group is pretty low, which means that it is intimate but the sample size is often unrepresentative. Quantitative research helps you to increase the sample size providing greater statistical significance. By including *demographic*, *psychographic* and even *firmographic* questions in your survey you can gather much of the information that you will need when making strategic and tactical decisions further down the line. You want to understand not just who your customers are but their attitudes, beliefs and behaviours. Don't underestimate the value of this information during the marketing process. If you want to develop an evidence based marketing strategy you need evidence to do it with.

If you are developing a first of its kind product or looking to pioneer a new, never before seen way of delivering pharmaceutical care, market research will have its limitations. It is excellent at exploring how your customers think and feel about things that already exist. It is less good in relation to exploring fine detail about the unknown. Even then however it can be useful as long as you are aware of the potential constraints and consider what you learn in that context.

Research actions

1. Define the gaps in your knowledge. What is it that you don't know and what kind of approach will best help you find the answers?

2. Carry out initial research based on secondary sources to find out what other people have already learnt.

3. Carry out further primary research to increase specificity and statistical significance including where relevant, focus groups and customer surveys. Be sure to involve participants who represent people who would purchase your product rather than a random sample.

Research notes

Case study | Step 1

Diagnostic

You have decided to review the clinical services that you provide and begin with your stop smoking service. While you have been providing an NHS commissioned service for a number of years, you have never provided a private service and want to explore whether that is viable or not. You and your team are experienced in delivering the NHS commissioned service and feel that you understand what works and what doesn't. Your local competitors also provide the NHS commissioned service.

Orientation

As the team leader you begin by recognising that your individual experience of delivering the NHS commissioned service affords you minimal information on which to base your service review. You experience the service from one side. Your side. You realise that you can't rely on guesswork about how your customers experience the service because your view as the provider is biased. You admit to yourself that despite best intentions you are often focused on operational tasks rather than customers and how to best satisfy them.

You take action and commit to understanding what the customer experience is really like. You consider a number of options. You could ask your team to deliver the service to you. You could ask a friend to use the service and report back. You could employ a professional mystery shopper. You decide to invest in the latter and a number of weeks later you have some feedback from multiple visits.

You now have a broad view of what your customers' experiences might be like and a number of obvious areas of improvement are clear. You plan a meeting with your team and talk about the review process, the feedback and how to make initial improvements. You share your new focus on customer satisfaction and the process you want to work through to improve how your NHS commissioned service is delivered and to check the viability of a private service. You ask for their commitment to customer satisfaction and contribution to the process.

Research

You can see the value in mystery shopper feedback about your current service but also recognise its limitations and that your customers will teach you the most.

You take action. You decide to hold two focus groups, each with around eight customers, to uncover the kind of issues that matter around stop smoking services. You recruit a group of customers who represent the users of your service and a group that don't use it but may benefit.

You plan to gather information about demographics, attitudes, beliefs and behaviours to inform the marketing process as you proceed.

The focus groups are enlightening and you learn a lot about what your customers think of your pharmacy in general, as well as about the stop smoking service. What matters to your customers becomes pretty clear. You learn why your current service users chose your pharmacy and you learn why those who don't use the service make that choice.

You are eager to learn more. Now that you understand some of the qualitative issues you want to understand the scale of those issues and whether they are important to the majority. You put together a short survey focussed around the issues that matter and share it with your customers in the pharmacy and online. You offer a small incentive to encourage people to respond. You calculate how many responses you need for you to be confident of your results and encourage your team to help you reach the target. You gather the data over a number of weeks. In the meantime you want to understand how your service differs from your competitors so you research what they offer and you update your knowledge of smoking cessation treatments to make sure you haven't missed anything.

When the survey data comes in, some of the issues raised in the focus groups are seen to be relevant to the majority while others are less so. You now understand what matters and how much. That is solid evidence upon which you can base development of your stop smoking services.

Step two

Step two looks at prescribing the specific group(s) you will target, which you will ignore and what you want to stand for in the mind of your customers.

Prescriptive

+ Segmentation
+ Targeting
+ Positioning

Research

● [Segmentation]

Targeting

Positioning

Segmentation

Segmentation looks at splitting the total market into distinct groups who value your product for their own reasons.

Ockham's razor and the pharmacy market

When people started marketing in the way that we would recognise now they did what we would call mass marketing. The same messages, materials and products for everyone. Over time, things have become more complicated and targeted marketing has become the accepted norm. Tailored messages, materials and products for groups of similar customers and even individuals.

There are currently two opposing theories within marketing academic circles about how we should characterise a market and how that influences the other aspects of our marketing strategy.

The first and until relatively recently (around 2010) the accepted theory, suggests that markets can be split into smaller, distinct groups that are the same within and different without. As a result it is believed that these different groups must have different needs, views and preferences, all of which should have an impact on how we design and deliver our products. This theory highlights the differences between people and is targeted marketing.

A competing theory has been put forward recently which suggests that people who are interested in a particular product should be defined by their behaviour rather than their characteristics. It suggests that apparent differences between groups who purchase the same product don't impact on how often or how extensively they buy that product and rather than target one particular group of customers, we should market to all customers who may be interested in our product. This theory highlights the similarities between people and is a return towards mass marketing.

Opposing academic camps make compelling arguments and I mention it here because the chosen theory drives many of the tactical decisions we make later in the marketing process. William of Ockham, a scholastic philosopher (1285-1347) left us with a principle which goes like this, 'Entities are not to be multiplied beyond necessity.' That is, keep it simple. It is useful to help us decide which marketing theory to use in which case. We should use the least complicated academic model that makes sense.

There are some clear groupings within the total market that pharmacies sell to. Only certain people will be interested in a weight management service. Equally only certain people will be interested in a stop smoking service. These are obvious functional groupings and they could be used to help guide our tactical choices. However even within these groupings it is conceivable that there are smaller groups. A 70 year old who is eligible for a healthy heart check on the NHS may respond to different marketing materials than a 45 year old with a family history. These groupings are based on characteristics rather than functions.

In other cases, where the appeal of a particular product is wider, for example supply of prescription medicines, taking the time and effort to develop and produce different marketing campaigns and materials may or may not be justified.

You will need to make a judgement of which theory is best applied in each instance when you are developing a strategy for your pharmacy or for individual products. It is a judgement which explores whether preparing different sets of marketing messages, materials and products for different target groups is likely to deliver a return on that investment or not. Your market research will help uncover whether there are distinct groups for whom this might be worthwhile.

Pharmacy customers certainly have different functional needs based on age, gender, condition etc and anyone who has worked in a pharmacy for any length of time will tell you that customers each have their own characteristics or personality. How significant these needs and traits are in terms of marketing segmentation depends on context.

While you deliberate over which side of the fence you fall, we will cover segmentation and targeting as part of our marketing process because they are useful when designing new products for a particular market, whether they are segmented by function, personality or behaviour and can help to decide which groups to ignore and in doing so focus precious resources.

Homogeneous and heterogeneous

Segmentation

Segmentation is the act of splitting a total market into groups who are similar or homogeneous within and dis-similar or heterogeneous without. Market research can often uncover previously unrecognised complexity within the market which can disorientate you. The complexity was always there. Segmentation helps to create order out of that chaos.

You can only appeal in an average way to an average customer. Not all customers are the same and they may purchase a given product for different reasons. When you have split your market into smaller groups it enables you to pick and choose how best to use your limited resources, to design communications that resonate more with specific groups and to maximise profit.

Good segmentation is an important step, built on the data gathered during your market research, that informs the selection of which segments to market to and how best to appeal to them.

Segment based on combined data

When you get it right segmentation is a powerful tool but it is easy to get it wrong and head off towards a dead end. Choose the data you use carefully. You need a mixture of different types of data to help you.

Demographic

Use the personal details information from your market research to understand who the people are that you want to market to and where you can reach them. A common demographic segmentation in the pharmacy market separates young mothers and seniors. This kind of information is most useful to help you choose which segment to market to.

Psychographic

Use the information about your sample's beliefs and attitudes to understand what your target market is thinking, what matters to them, by how much and how you can influence their behaviour. A common segmentation in the pharmacy market separates people who think of pharmacy as healthcare and those who think of it as retail. This kind of information is most useful to help you choose how to present your product or service to your customers.

Behavioural

Combine behavioural information with psychographic to understand what is driving your target segment's actions. People say one thing but do another so behavioural information is critical. A common segmentation in the pharmacy market separates those who use your pharmacy and those who don't! This kind of information is most useful to help you determine what messages to communicate about your product or service.

Don't feel like segmentation always has to result in identifying multiple segments. It is about unearthing what is already there rather than creating something new. If there are no meaningful segments in your total market then fine. It makes your life less complex.

'Market segmentation is a natural result of the vast differences among people'.

Donald Norman, Director, The Design Lab, University of California

It's easier to hit a bigger target

When you have separated your total market into smaller homogeneous groups it is important to try and put some numbers against them so that you know how big each group is. What may appear a really attractive segment initially might be revealed to be a route to ruin.

Use your information about the total size of the market and assess as accurately as possible what proportion of that market each segment represents, how many individual customers that is, how much each might spend over a given time period and hence the total monetary value of that segment. Compare the monetary value with the number of individuals. A segment with a huge monetary value but with thousands of individuals might be really hard to convert and therefore not as attractive as it at first seems. Your Medicines Use Review segment is small and capped but high value per individual. Your Electronic Prescription Service segment is much larger and only limited by patient list size but with a lower value per individual. Which one you focus on first is a matter of prioritisation.

If your numbers can be accurate, great, but they don't have to be 100% perfect. Don't let pin point accuracy be a barrier to valuing segments. It is an important and useful step. This is about broad decisions and there is often enough space between valuations of different segments that it is crystal clear which are the most attractive, even given room for error.

Fig 2. Healthcare market size

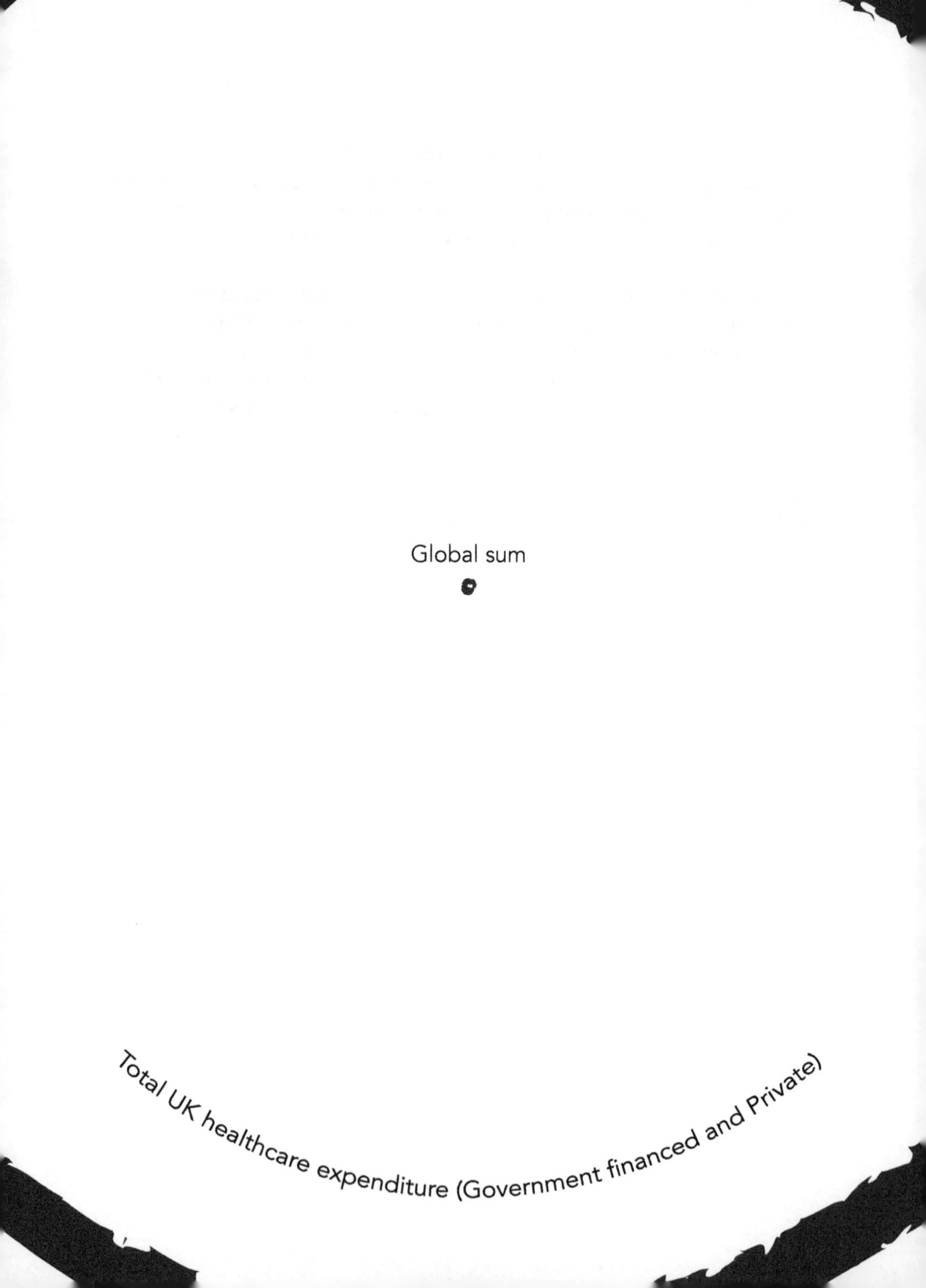

Global sum

Total UK healthcare expenditure (Government financed and Private)

Market size

A key element of the marketing challenge is to develop a product that delivers value for the highest number of people. The larger the market size the higher the potential sales and the more profit you can make. This is a really important marketing goal for most companies.

Everyone needs pharmacy services. Some more than others but the total market size is the national population. While that population is growing the total market size is not the critical factor where pharmacy is concerned, unlike many other sectors. The NHS is our dominant paymaster and has a profound effect on our view of market size. Where core pharmacy NHS services are concerned, the value of the total market is fixed in the form of the global sum. As pharmacists we need to focus on growing our market share within this global sum. To exceed the capped market size presented by the standard NHS contract we also need to look outside of it and develop products that satisfy the needs of others who are willing to pay for them. That may be other NHS funding or private.

Total healthcare expenditure in the UK, both Government funded and private is close to 100 times the global sum. Around 1/5th of it is private. Something to think about when considering your market.

Equally unusual is that our paymaster doesn't decide whether to use our service at the point of care. Individual customers do. Due to their specific needs and the funding structure not all patients are equal. At least, not as equally profitable. The national contract requires pharmacies to provide services to every patient whether that is highly profitable or loss making. You can decide to pro-actively pursue specific, highly profitable patient groups if you choose to do so. There is no rule against that.

Segmentation actions

1. Identify key traits within your total market, both functional and characteristic, using the data collected during your market research.

2. Identify groupings within your total market based on combinations of these characteristics.

3. Test the groupings you have identified based upon internal similarities and external differences compared with other groupings.

Segmentation notes

esearch

Segmentation

[Targeting]

Positioning

Targeting

Targeting looks at choosing which segments to market to and which to ignore.

The first strategic decision

Choose which segment or segments to target and you have made your first strategic marketing decision. So far the marketing process has been all about the market. Understanding them, quantifying their preferences and separating them into groups that mean something and that we can act upon. Targeting is the first time that you look inwards and consider your pharmacy.

Don't be tempted to begin targeting until you have segmented the whole market. In the race to act you might miss out on a great opportunity if you have only a partial segmentation. Don't purely focus on which segments to target. Flip the coin and actively consider which market segments to ignore. This might seem paradoxical. You want to sell as much as possible to as many as possible. However, even the biggest companies in the world have a limit to their resources and your pharmacy almost certainly does. For that reason you need to make some choices about what to offer to whom and how to promote it, that fit within your resources and maximise your return on investment.

That is targeting.

The benefits of targeting

Targeting enables the most efficient use of resources. Even though it may not seem like it you have an almost endless number of options about what to offer, to whom and targeting based on good segmentation, allows you to work out which of those options is likely to generate the most profit.

By selecting a segment and more importantly ignoring other segments you can tailor your offer to appeal strongly to your target segment without watering it down by worrying about appealing to the mass market. Picking a specific group of people to sell to enables you to position your offer directly to those people and against a smaller number of competitors.

You can often reduce the number of competitors by ignoring certain segments which might be attractive to other brands. Fewer competitors, more opportunity. Don't forget that competitors for your pharmacy come from outside the profession as well as within.

Targeting one segment this year does not mean that you can't choose to target a different one next year so don't fret too much about what you feel you might be missing out on. The work you do to market to a specific segment often spills over into other adjoining segments creating additional value for no additional work.

Fig 3. Choosing a target segment: Criteria

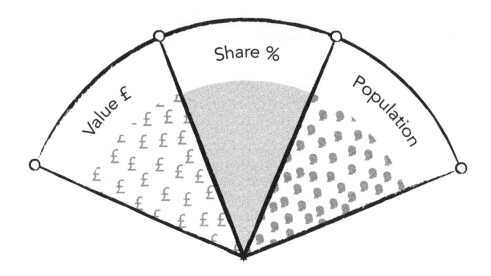

How to choose a target segment

A good segmentation often makes the choice of a target segment really obvious. It will jump off the page. For the times when this isn't the case select a target based on the following criteria.

Monetary value

You have worked out how much each segment is worth already. Higher value segments are a good place to start and warrant further analysis.

Current share

If you already have a 50% market share of a particular segment it may take more work to convert the remaining 50%, than picking a segment where you have only 5% market share and more opportunity.

Consider your product. Look for a segment that suits your product better than other segments. If you can't find one select a new segment or develop your product.

Population

Depending on the context you may prefer a higher population as there are more potential customers or a lower population because there will be less work involved in converting them into customers. If two segments of the same monetary value have a population of 100 and 500 it will be more demanding to convince 500 individuals to make a purchase than it will to convince 100. This doesn't mean it's not worth it, it just means that you should be aware of it when targeting.

'Talent hits a target no one else can hit. Genius hits a target no one else can see.'

Arthur Schopenhauer, German Philosopher

Describe your target segment

Write a *segment portrait* which answers the question 'Who is the customer?' This will enable you to keep them in mind when making decisions about how to market your product. For each target segment you'll need to write an individual segment portrait. If you think one portrait covers more than one segment then you have learnt that your segmentation wasn't quite right and you should collapse the two segments to form a single one.

There are a few key areas to think about when writing a segment portrait. Who the customer is in demographic terms, what they currently think, what they actually do in relation to your product, what gets them excited and what puts them off. Make sure that you are not overly positive. Try to be realistic as this will produce a much more useful portrait. A lot of the data you gathered during your market research will be useful in helping you describe your customer.

A customer who uses your prescription delivery service because they are elderly and housebound would be described very differently to a customer who uses it because they are a busy single parent. How you market your products to them could differ significantly.

Targeting actions

1. Determine the total population of each segment and their purchasing habits.

2. Calculate the potential monetary value of each segment and your current market share.

3. Select which segments represent the most attractive opportunity and which you will target first.

Targeting notes

mentation

Targeting

[Positioning]

trics

Positioning

Positioning looks at what you want to stand for in the minds of your customers.

Positioning your pharmacy

Determining what you would like to stand for in the mind of your customers is an exciting step in the development of your marketing strategy. Your choice should appeal directly to your chosen target segment. Any one product or brand i.e. your whole pharmacy, can be positioned in an almost limitless number of ways. The positioning of individual products will sit within the framework of your overall brand positioning and should complement it.

You may choose to position your pharmacy based on speed of service, location, opening hours, range of services or a whole host of other attributes. It's important not to get carried away. People won't remember more than two or three attributes and you should work hard to become associated with those.

Positioning is often called different things by different people. Values, mission statements, purpose, personality to name a few. They all mean the same thing and relate to a short list of what you want to be known for. It doesn't really matter what you call it as long as you keep it concise and oversimplify the messages to help create the associations in the mind of the customer.

How you position your pharmacy will influence many of the tactical marketing decisions that follow.

The two aims of positioning

When positioning your pharmacy the aims are very simple. Your customer should know that you exist and they should hold in their mind two or three key associations when they think about you. Positioning is to do with memory. Your customers' memory. You want to be in their mind when it occurs to them that they need pharmaceutical care and you want them to have some positive associations or memories that remind them that they want to use your pharmacy.

You don't apply positioning to your product. It is not something you do to it. It is something that you do to the mind of your customer. If you claim to offer fast service in all of your communications but you take longer than your competitors, your customers will quickly pick up on this.

Making sure that your customers know you are there is winning a position in their minds. Selecting and building two or three key associations is the act of influencing what that position is and how it affects their behaviour towards your pharmacy. Some customers may value friendliness over location and so on. There is no universally right position, only a position that is right for your pharmacy and your target segment.

Creating a memory can be quite quick but people forget just as quickly, so refreshing and maintaining those memories in your customers' minds is one of the key jobs of your marketing communications. It takes time but it's worth it.

Would you rather that your customers forget about your pharmacy?

Fig 4. The three Cs of positioning

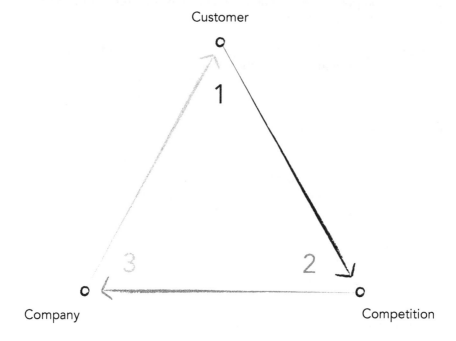

The three Cs of positioning

When selecting your position, base it firstly on the customer, then your competitors and finally on your company. In that order.

Customer

Position your product by highlighting how it meets the most important customer needs.

Competitor

Research your competitors and assess what they are saying are their strongest points. Position your product in opposition. If they offer 'national coverage' offer 'local service' to be different. If an attribute is essential point out that you match their offer.

Company

Finally make sure that you can consistently deliver what you have claimed as your position. Don't overreach. If you can't deliver it, pick a different association rather than fail your customers. It will be hard to win them back.

If you can find a position that delivers what the customer wants consistently and either better than or differently to your competitors you will improve your chances of long term success.

'Differentiate or die.'

Jack Trout, Author, Marketing Consultant

Differentiation vs distinctiveness

For your marketing communications to have the best chance of working, customers firstly have to notice them and secondly they have to recognise that it is your pharmacy that is behind the messages. This sounds simple. Obvious almost but so often it goes wrong and these basic links are broken, rendering communications pointless. When you consider the number of marketing messages that an individual is exposed to during any 24 hour period it's clear that their attention will be fragmented at best and absent at worst.

Marketers spend a lot of time thinking about the best way to win customers' attention amidst the visual and mental noise of daily life. There are two main approaches taken.

Differentiation

Literally to appear different. Different to your competitors that is.

By highlighting ways in which your pharmacy is in some way superior (within legal, ethical and professional constraints) you might aim to provide a reason for customers to choose your pharmacy for their care. Differentiation is closely linked with positioning and it is often around the chosen positioning attributes that differences are highlighted.

Differentiation alone relies on your customers being interested enough to engage with your brand and your competitors' brands at a level sufficient to recognise the differences you are aiming to communicate. As you can imagine this requires some effort on the part of your customer and is not guaranteed. More than that, some believe that the vast majority of customers just aren't engaged at that level.

'Rather than striving for meaningful, perceived differentiation, marketers should seek meaningless distinctiveness.'

Byron Sharp, Professor of Marketing Science, University of South Australia

Distinctiveness

Literally to appear distinct. Distinct from your competitors that is.

By working to develop visual and verbal identities that are distinct from your competitors and applying them as consistently as possible you might aim to ensure that your communications are always identifiable.

Despite the aspirations of brand managers people almost always place category above brand. That is they will almost always think 'I need a painkiller' before 'I need a [particular brand of painkiller]', unless the marketing team for the branded version have done a particularly good job. Being unmistakable in your category is a highly valuable asset.

Distinctiveness alone relies on your customers making purchase choices based on a much lower level of engagement than brand owners expect. People often purchase based on what they recognise, are familiar with and have purchased previously.

There are those that believe in differentiation. There are those that believe in distinctiveness. Luckily we don't have to choose only one approach.

When marketing your pharmacy, work on your positioning and differentiate your brand. There is value in that. Communicate these differences. Also work on your visual and verbal identity and make sure that it is distinct from your competitors. Then apply it consistently. Every time. You can benefit from both.

Fig 5. The benefit ladder

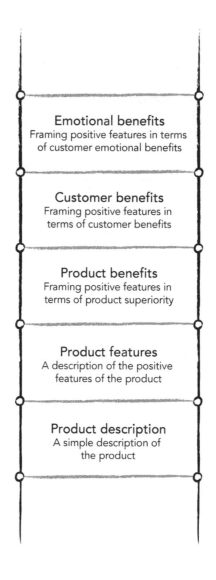

Emotional benefits
Framing positive features in terms
of customer emotional benefits

Customer benefits
Framing positive features in
terms of customer benefits

Product benefits
Framing positive features in
terms of product superiority

Product features
A description of the positive
features of the product

Product description
A simple description of
the product

Features and benefits

It is often said that people don't buy features, they buy benefits. This is based on a concept called the Benefit ladder which is a tool to help you develop how you position your product. Move any given positioning attribute up the ladder (start at the bottom) and you may have a more compelling position with your target segment. Let's think about this book as an example.

+ **Product description.** A pile of paper glued together with marketing related words and images printed on them.

+ **Product features.** A concise, easy to read book, containing marketing advice and a step by step application process for pharmacy people.

+ **Product benefits.** Specialist marketing advice for pharmacists by a pharmacist, providing tailored insights and clear actions.

+ **Customer benefits.** Understand and apply proven marketing processes to help your pharmacy business grow.

+ **Emotional benefits.** Feel like you are better prepared than your competition and that you have discovered a way to compete and win.

This process can be applied when positioning your pharmacy as a whole or a particular product. Of course some customers love detail and that can be provided too but positioning is about key associations in the minds of the customer not detail. That comes later.

Be careful not to get carried away. There has been a tendency for brands to try and engineer a higher purpose for what are, at times, mundane everyday products in an attempt to move up the ladder and align themselves with something that people genuinely care about. It is sometimes called Brand purpose. This can often be transparent and a little embarrassing for the brand if they are challenged on the authenticity of it. If you genuinely have a deeper purpose that you can articulate well and makes sense then use it. It is like gold. If you don't, keep it realistic.

Positioning actions

1. Explore your pharmacy's strengths and your competitors' weaknesses in the context of your customers' needs.

2. Select two or three of these attributes that position your pharmacy competitively.

3. Build and maintain associations with these attributes through your tactical choices and the use of distinctive visual and verbal identity.

Positioning notes

Case study | Step two

Prescriptive

Using your market research you want to really understand who your stop smoking customers are, their needs, how you can satisfy them and how you can develop your service to appeal to them.

Segmentation

You analyse the data you have collected and see that there are different natural groupings within the overall market for stop smoking services. You assumed that being a smoker was a hard and fast criteria but you've realised that non-smokers who want their loved ones to quit might be worth thinking about too. There are those who literally couldn't afford to pay for a private service and there are those who could. There are those who can visit your pharmacy during standard opening hours and there are those who can't because they are less mobile or because they work long hours. There are those who have never tried to quit and there are those who have tried everything possible.

Now that you think about it, the market appears much more complex than you thought. It was always like that. You are beginning to understand it fully. By carefully looking at the characteristics of different customers you start to see some clear groupings that may be relevant.

- Non-smokers who want their loved ones to quit
- Smokers who use your current stop smoking service
- Smokers who don't use your current stop smoking service
- Smokers who have tried everything to quit
- Smokers who have never tried to quit
- Smokers from a lower sociodemographic group who want support from the NHS
- Smokers from a higher sociodemographic group who are willing to pay for support

You share your analysis with others in your team and gather their thoughts. You test how robust your segmentation is by confirming internal similarities within the groups and external differences between the groups.

You realise that some people belong to more than one group. You make sure that your segmentation is based on meaningful differences. That is, the characteristics you use to segment have an influence on buying behaviour. Non-smokers won't access your service directly but they might influence the buying behaviour of others. Smokers from a lower sociodemographic group might not pay for private support and are more likely to access the NHS commissioned service.

You also consider how easy it might be to communicate with a particular group. You look for obvious ways to reach them that are within the constraints of your resources.

Targeting

You start deciding which segments to target and in what order. You would like to grow sales as much as possible but realise that your marketing budget is limited and you want to focus first on where you might make the best return on investment.

You combine secondary research with your own market research to gather data about how many people might be in each of your segments. You multiply that by the monetary value of each person who might access your service. For the NHS commissioned service you will have data about remuneration and quit rates. To explore the potential of a private service you might multiply the number of people by a range of different prices that you could charge to gain an understanding and assess viability. You adjust for your current market share and how hard it would be to convince people in a particular segment.

You realise that while the non-smokers segment is big in terms of the number of people, each person has no direct value. You choose not to market to this segment initially.

You realise that to maximise the value of smokers who use your current service you can work on improving quit rate. You choose not to market to this segment initially but make a note to review how to achieve better quit rates when looking at service delivery later in the marketing process.

You realise that smokers in a lower sociodemographic group are an important target segment for the NHS commissioned service. You choose to target both those who have never tried to quit and those who have tried everything. You give the segments descriptive names so that you and your team can refer to them easily:

- Low sociodemographic never tried
- Low sociodemographic tried it all

You realise that smokers in a higher sociodemographic group are also a target segment for the NHS commissioned service and that they are also a potential target segment for a new private service. You choose to target both those who have never tried to quit and those who have tried everything. You give the segments descriptive names so that you and your team can refer to them easily:

- High sociodemographic never tried
- High sociodemographic tried it all

You have narrowed down your focus, clarified who you are targeting and confirmed the viability of a private stop smoking service. Great progress.

You write a segment profile for each of the four target segments to develop a clear picture in your mind of who you are marketing to. You thought ahead so the focus group and survey data will come in handy here.

Positioning

Using your segment profiles you start to work on how you will position the NHS commissioned and the private stop smoking services.

Your NHS commissioned service is offered by your local competitors but your review of their services has uncovered that their provision is patchy based on availability of accredited staff, their consultation rooms are poorly fitted out and their quit rates are significantly lower than yours

You decide to position your NHS commissioned service based on availability five days a week, a professional environment and the high success rates enjoyed by your service users.

You have realised that a real barrier to access for the higher sociodemographic group is being able to visit the pharmacy during opening hours. Your research into the latest developments in smoking cessation have found a new treatment that is not on offer through the NHS commissioned service.

You decide to position your private service as one of a kind in your area, conveniently available out of standard opening hours and providing access to the latest smoking cessation treatments.

MARKETING
SOLUTION
(CONCENTRATED)

Step three

Step three looks at defining the right marketing goals at the right time.

Objective

+ Goal setting

Set your goals

It may seem like a strange point at which to mention setting goals. You set your goals at the start, right? Strategic considerations come even before goal setting, at least they do where marketing goals are concerned. Before we dive headlong into tactical considerations it is worth taking the time to work on your goals.

Setting goals is a skill. Set the right goals and frame them correctly and you are a lot closer to achieving them. Don't just decide in some vague fashion that you want more sales and expect your marketing to deliver that. That would be like expecting a randomly selected tablet to treat an illness just because it is a tablet. Firstly take the aspirational vision you developed, think about where you are going to play and how you are going to win, then think about specific marketing goals that will help you get there.

Be SMART. Specific, Measured, Achievable, Relevant and Timed. Make sure that you frame your objectives using this well known approach and you will find that you have written something that you can actually use in practice.

Come back to this section when you've absorbed most of the ideas in this book and write three or four key marketing goals for the next twelve months. If you have enough resource, write a couple more.

Many of the ideas we are looking at present a potential marketing goal for your pharmacy.

For example, when you have selected a target segment for your new clinical service, you will have defined your market share percentage. A SMART goal may be to increase your market share to a specific percentage over a specific time.

Equally, when you have built your integrated marketing communications plan (we'll cover this later) you will have a schedule of activity that you have decided will do the job. A SMART goal may be to implement every element of the plan consistently, to a defined quality standard, according to the schedule.

Not all objectives are equal however! It is important to decide the point in the customer journey at which you want your marketing to act. You may want to raise awareness of your pharmacy in the local or wider community. On the other hand you may be happy with the level of awareness and want more people to seriously consider using your pharmacy rather than their current one. Or perhaps you have already worked on this and now want to convince people to purchase a particular product.

The particular approach to achieving these different goals could vary significantly so be sure that you are clear on what you are aiming for before you start.

Educate then sell

In pharmacy we consider ourselves to be providers of pharmaceutical care. Healthcare professionals who deliver personalised advice and care on a daily basis to over a million people. This is our calling. This is our purpose. It is what we would like people to recall when they think of us. It is our positioning. It is our brand.

Most of society go along with our self-image in the main but perhaps not to the extent that we would like. Brand owners always care much more deeply about their brand than others do. Society recognises us in some capacity as providing a useful function. However, most of them don't think any more about it and don't really care as long as they can get their medicines when they need them. Sadly that is the truth of it. We will always care more about pharmacy than people outside of the profession do.

That said, they know what they know about us and we can use that understanding to our advantage when marketing. Most people expect pharmacies to sell medicines, dispense prescriptions and provide advice about how to use them. Those are the solid, no argument associations held by the vast majority and that have built up over decades, perhaps longer. They are a huge, market based asset at the disposal of pharmacists, individual pharmacies and the profession as a whole.

So we can safely expect to be able to promote these services as much as we like without needing to explain ourselves. People will know what we are selling and will either choose to purchase or not based on a pretty good understanding of what it is, how much it costs, whether that is good value, how it compares to elsewhere they can get it and whether they need it at the time.

We currently hit the buffers when we step outside of these known areas and for obvious reasons. People don't expect us to provide other healthcare services. Despite our best efforts in recent years. Not in large numbers that would make a difference. When we start selling these services people understandably get confused. It's not what they expect and they don't understand the offering so they can't assess its value. They leave it there.

What can you do in your pharmacy? Work hard to reinforce the solid associations that people already have. Be a pharmacy. Don't be a department store, or a gift shop or a discount retailer. Then anticipate the need to educate customers regarding new services that don't fit into their expectations before you can start selling to them. This may take time and will certainly take some thought.

Your initial marketing goal may be to educate customers rather than to furiously sell to them. It's hard to sell what people don't understand and they are unlikely to buy what they don't expect you to be selling.

'People don't care about your business. They care about their problems. Be the solution they are looking for.'

Mental and physical availability

You spend what seems like every waking hour working in or thinking about your pharmacy. Your customer on the other hand may spend five or ten minutes a month in your pharmacy and only think of you fleetingly otherwise. That is a big difference and an important one. While your pharmacy is one of the most important considerations in your life, it is almost inconsequential to your customers. With a few exceptions they need you when they need you and otherwise you are out of mind.

While you may think that it is the loyal, regular customers that you need to focus on, it isn't. They've already made the decision to come to you. They may bring more value to your business as individuals but there are fewer of them than there are of the occasional customers who use a range of pharmacies. Think about both but focus more on occasional customers.

It starts with a need

A customer needs pharmaceutical care. They run down the list of places they can access that care. For your loyal customers you may be dominant in that list, perhaps the only one, and they will come to you. For the occasional customers their list will differ. It might not even include all of the pharmacies in the area. It is unlikely to. They will know the pharmacies that they know and will pick from that list which suits them best for a range of reasons that day.

A key marketing goal is to be part of that list in your customers mind. As many customers as possible. If you aren't in the list they can't pick you. This is mental availability. This is brand *salience*.

Some believe that the main aim of marketing communications is to increase and maintain mental availability. To make it into the list and to rank as highly as possible in that list because of the associations and memories that customers have. It takes a long time which is why marketing activity is often charged with being ineffective. An advert should lead to a sale right? Perhaps, but it should definitely contribute to building an association and a reminder of your pharmacy. The sale may occur in a day, a month or longer.

Fig 6. Mental availability

Loyal customer

Occasional customer

Non-customer

It ends with a purchase

You rank as first choice for a particular customer on a particular day. Great. However, they can only make a purchase if you are physically available. If you aren't available they can't make a purchase. This is physical availability.

Having a number of pharmacies across a tight geographical area helps but it is not the only factor. Having the right location, the right travel links, the right parking, the right shops and services next to your pharmacy, the right opening hours and the right online services all matter too.

Think about which goals will help you build and maintain mental availability and maximise your physical availability.

Goal setting actions

1. Start with your aspirational vision.

2. Read and review all of the ideas in this book.

3. Define three specific SMART marketing goals that will help you achieve your aspirational vision.

Marketing goal number one

Marketing goal number two

Marketing goal number three

Goal setting notes

Case study | Step three

Objective

You decide that your aspirational goal is to help the people in your community live more healthily by delivering high quality stop smoking services that meet their needs at a profit.

+ Your primary goal for your NHS commissioned service is to increase your market share from 36% to 56% over a twelve month period.

To help achieve this you set yourself some smaller goals.

+ To raise understanding of lifestyle factors in relation to health, specifically smoking, from 52% to 64% over a twelve month period.

+ To raise awareness of the service in the minds of your customers from 56% to 80% over a twelve month period.

+ To re-position the service in the minds of your customers based on your new positioning attributes from 12% to 65% over the a twelve month period.

You thought ahead so you have data from your market research that tells you what your starting points are. You can measure again in twelve months.

You recognise the importance of goal setting, discuss and share the goals with your team. You are ready to consider how you will achieve these goals through the tactical choices you make

Tactical execution

The pharmacy profession must catch up with the rest of the world and become expert marketing tacticians. We are all busy so this may seem impossible but it is not a choice, it is an imperative. Great tactical execution relies on judging which combination of tactical choices will have the desired effect, mastering the techniques required to implement those choices, monitoring the results and adjusting for continuous improvement. This is the tactical cycle. Where changes in the environment overtake adaptation there is only one outcome for those failing to adapt.

Tactical choices

Tactics is the work that helps us implement our strategy and to answer detailed questions about how we design and deliver products that will appeal to our target market.

+ What is my product?
+ Are there any ways that I can make it more appealing?
+ How much should I charge?
+ How should I distribute my product?
+ How should I tell customers about my product?
+ How can I influence my customer experience?

There are two steps. They will help you answer some of those questions in more detail.

+ Step four | Product design
+ Step five | Product delivery

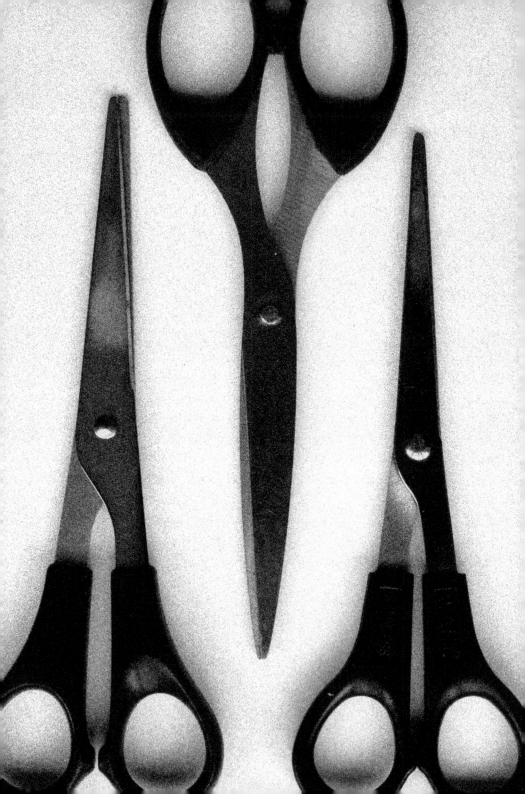

Step four

Step four looks at product design through the four Ps of marketing. Product, Price, Place and Promotion are the first considerations when applying your brand position and building an offer that appeals to your target segment. We will look at each in some detail.

Product design

+ Product
+ Price
+ Place
+ Promotion

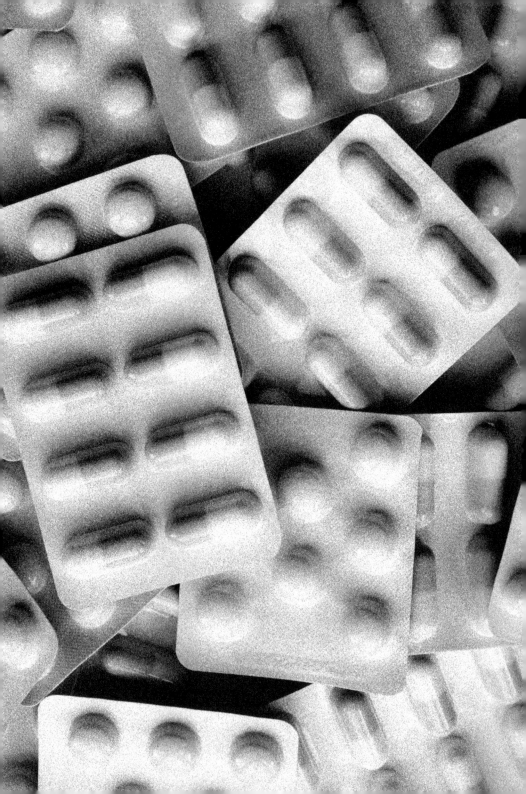

The 4 Ps of marketing

You can present a single product in a wide range of different ways that match the specific needs of any given target segment. The product remains the same but the way it appears differs. The 4 Ps model is the framework that enables you to design a product offering.

Decisions are made in each of the four areas and the overall result is the offer your customer sees. While you can work through the four Ps in any order, a decision in any one P affects the others and may require adjustment of decisions you have already made. Start with the Product P.

When an organisation gets carried away and distorts claims about how a product meets a customers' needs, problems arise for both the organisation and the customer. A theoretical example might be claiming that a flu vaccine is quadrivalent when in fact the vaccine in hand is trivalent. This kind of activity is sadly not uncommon outside of the pharmacy profession and has reflected badly on marketing as a discipline. Marketing is just a tool however.

It is the intentions of the marketer and the way in which they use the tool which determines the effect. As pharmacists we must always aim to market ourselves, our organisations and our products without distortion. Our services are valuable enough that they will be well received without resorting to such practices.

Originally modelled in their current form by Jerome McCarthy in his 1960 textbook, Basic Marketing: A Managerial Approach, the continued value of the 4 Ps model has been questioned in recent times. Half a century has passed and people who are caught up in the tactical implementation of marketing at the expense of strategic concerns mistakenly believe that changes to how we communicate render the model irrelevant.

The customer is at the heart of each P. While the customer matters the 4 Ps will matter. When considering each of the Ps, focus on how you can satisfy your customer and you won't go far wrong. The cumulative effect across everything you do and how you do it is pretty powerful.

Metrics

[Product] ●

Price

Product

Product looks at the characteristics of what you want to sell and how to perfect them.

'A product is anything that can be offered to a market for attention, acquisition, use or consumption.'

Philip Kotler, Professor of International Marketing, Kellogg School of Management, Northwestern University

Definition of a product

While in pharmacy we tend to think of a product as a physical item that a customer may purchase over the counter, the marketing definition is different: 'A product is anything that can be offered to a market for attention, acquisition, use or consumption.' (Kotler, P).

This definition is important as it allows us to consider the wide range of retail products and services that pharmacies offer in the same terms. With the counselling we provide at the point of sale and the treatments we provide as part of many services the lines are blurred and this definition provides clarity.

Throughout this book where I have used the term product I am using it based on the above definition. Whether you are thinking about a 16p pack of generic paracetamol or an advanced, one of a kind clinical service you can use the same approach to determine how best to present the product to your customer. It will naturally be less complex for the paracetamol compared to the service in which case adapt your efforts accordingly.

Fig 7. The three product dimensions

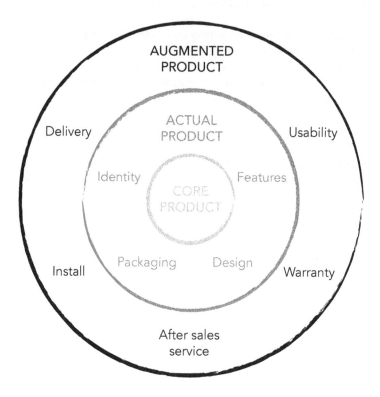

Three product dimensions

When developing a product think about three different dimensions. The core product, the actual product and the augmented product. Work out how to construct and combine these three dimensions to develop a product that best meets your customers' needs.

Core product

The core product is the dimension of the product that delivers the main benefit to the customer. Ibuprofen tablets reduce inflammation, pain and temperature. These are the core benefits.

Actual product

The actual product is the tangible dimension of the product. The shape, size, smell, texture, taste and colour of the ibuprofen. The blister pack they come in. The quality and design of the packaging. All of these will have an impact on the way the product is perceived by the customer. This may be what you traditionally think of as a product and is the dimension that customers come into direct contact with the most.

Augmented product

The augmented product is the experiential dimension that surrounds the purchase. Pre-sales communications (adverts etc) designed to add meaning to the product beyond the core benefit, the experience of accessing the product and post-sales support. The reputation of your pharmacy, the environment, ease of access, relationships with your team, counselling and your support with ongoing care amongst many other things are all part of the augmented product dimension.

Think about how your latest clinical service idea would look if you split it down into these areas. How would you define each dimension of your product? How could you enhance each of them to make the product more appealing, to make it superior to competitors' products and to make it satisfy customer needs better?

A product is a journey

Your customer starts on their journey to purchasing a product way before you become aware of it. You have mapped out the individual moments on their journey (touchpoints) to understand how you can aim to enhance your overall product by improving each moment already. If you didn't start with 'Customer realises they need xyz' your customer may have started before you and you might have missed something.

Customers start by recognising a need. They have a headache for example. They make a decision about how best to deal with that. Maybe they start with having a drink, or some food. If it persists they might move onto which product they believe will best treat the headache and where they prefer to source that product based on their prior experience. Some may do some research to update their knowledge of things that matter to them, like price, effectiveness, mode of action etc. Many may choose where to purchase based on their schedule for the day and which sources they may be near. There are a whole host of factors that will come into play which you will have explored during your market research.

The challenge is to design a three dimensional product that beats your competitors sufficiently to compel customers to come to your pharmacy and make a purchase. You have an opportunity to do this at each moment on the customer journey. Put some thought into what might work best and take action from the beginning of their journey, not part way through.

With the painkiller example it is not going to be the actual painkiller (the core product) because they can buy those almost anywhere. It is not going to be the packaging (the actual product) as many of the same products will be available in a range of locations. If you want customers to come to your pharmacy to purchase a painkiller you'll need to convince them through the augmented product dimension. Professional advice, wider range, better service, clinical environment etc.

Brand extension vs line extension

Be sure to develop products that align with your brand positioning and build your brand rather than striking out in an unexpected direction and risk damaging your brand.

The practice of pharmacy is continuously evolving and the products we offer evolve with it. Extemporaneous dispensing used to be common, now it is not. Our consultative and diagnostic services have expanded dramatically in recent years. Now we are exploring the challenges and opportunities offered by remote delivery online. Personalised medicines may be around the corner. Many factors push and pull us to develop new products. Selecting the right kind of products is essential to protect and build your brand and to give customers confidence in the credibility of your offer. This is even more critical for pharmacists as we do all of this within a professional context.

A brand extension is the offer of a product in a new category. This may be a service to support customers with their mental health. For many customers this could seem like a credible offer based upon their view of pharmacy itself, your particular brand and what it is competent at. For others they may not see the association based on their personal experience of pharmacy. A brand extension could also be a laser eye surgery service. It is safe to say that the majority of customers would not see this new offer as credible. It may be a stretch too far. Make sure that any new product that you develop aligns with your existing brand and is supported by your customers' associations with it. Building new associations often requires a lot of effort and time. It is possible but it is higher risk.

A line extension is the offer of a product of a different quality within the same category. This may be a new premium delivery service that includes delivery of retail products, collection of unwanted medicines and an assessment of housebound patients' wellbeing. A small charge could be applied, signifying higher quality. There is less risk of customer confusion as the service is well understood however the potential return may be variable depending on uptake.

'Don't find customers for your products, find products for your customers.'

Seth Godin, Author

Satisfiers, dissatisfiers and delighters

Your primary goal is customer satisfaction. Let's not forget that. When designing your product, all three dimensions, think about what aspects of that product will satisfy your customer, whether there are any that might be dissatisfying and if you can build in an aspect that delights them.

Looking in a little more detail at how your product delivers satisfaction can be worthwhile and help you to create or improve a product. Pharmacies operate in a competitive environment with new external competitors threatening the space. Making sure that you scrutinise every aspect of your products, maximise and highlight the satisfying aspects and minimise the dissatisfying aspects. This is an important step in response to these threats.

Developing your product to include new and unexpected benefits that are of real tangible value to your customers is one way to set your product apart. These benefits are sometimes called delighters. They are often related to how the product is delivered, that is the augmented product dimension rather than the actual product and are very much within the reach of pharmacies to develop.

In the rush to capture market share, prescription delivery services were developed by some pharmacies. When first provided these services were delighters. They provided a great reason for customers to choose the pharmacies that offered them. Over time the number of pharmacies offering delivery services grew and they became commonplace. Customers were used to them. They were the norm. They were no longer delighters, they were satisfiers at best. In fact, pharmacies that didn't offer delivery were at a significant disadvantage. The lack of delivery was a dissatisfier. It became essential for any pharmacy that wanted to compete effectively to offer a delivery service despite the, at times, variable financial return compared to a supply made without the costs of delivery.

Product actions

1. Consider each of the three product dimensions and define ways in which you can enhance your product for your customer.

2. Plot the product journey and map out how you can improve customer satisfaction at each point.

3. Keep an eye on the competition and respond to product improvements by matching or exceeding.

Product notes

ND 〈 Product ○

⌐

[Price]

●

e

CATION

Price

Price looks at matching the amount you charge to the value your customer perceives in your product.

Product drives price drives perception

When you develop your product, think about building in as much customer value as possible which will enable you to charge a higher price. In turn a higher price creates a perception of value. Value creation doesn't always have to cost you more money. Be creative.

Customers are happy to pay an amount that is equal to or less than the value they perceive in a product. This is crucial to understand. They base their judgement on perception not reality. You need to understand their perception. Value is at the heart of marketing.

A commodity is a generic equivalent indistinguishable from any other. We recognise this based on generic medicines. They are sold based upon price. Different providers try to undercut each other to capture market share. Brands are generally the opposite. They compete based upon meaning that adds value and do everything they can to maximise the perceived value of their product so that they can charge the highest price that the customer will pay. We get confused and frustrated when a customer perceives meaning in a generic medicine and will only accept a particular branded generic as a result.

Pharmacy is a profession, the status of which signifies quality. Do everything you can to communicate your professionalism and to drive that perception so that your customers perceive the real value of your products and you can charge a price that fairly reflects that value.

Compete with the supermarkets and discounters purely on price and you will be in a race to the bottom.

Pricing is the moment of truth.

You will learn whether your offer is good or whether you've missed something crucial in your marketing strategy.

The four profit factors

In the simplest terms there are four factors that drive profit. Units sold, unit price, fixed costs and variable costs. You already know them well. Unit price is the most powerful at affecting profit out of the four. Work hard to justify charging a unit price that delivers a healthy profit.

+ Increasing units sold has a positive effect on profitability but it is offset by an increase in variable costs (cost of goods).

+ Increasing unit price has a positive effect on profitability and doesn't result in an increase in fixed costs or variable costs.

+ Decreasing fixed costs has a positive effect on profitability but it is limited if sales do not grow.

+ Decreasing variable costs has a positive effect on profitability but it is not as easy to control as unit price.

Work on all of them, but focus most on justifying the maximum fair unit price. Your profitability will grow.

Fig 8. The value pricing thermometer

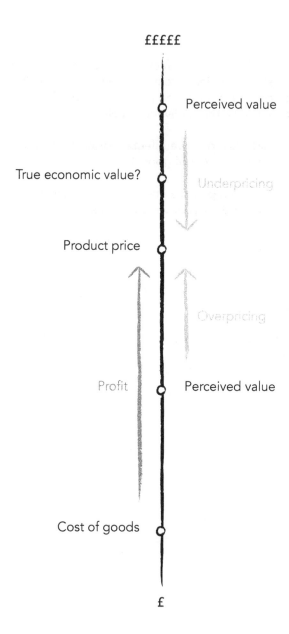

Pricing your product

When you are pricing a new product you can choose to start with your costs and add a percentage or price based on your understanding of how much value your customers perceive in your product and aim to match your price to that as closely as possible.

Beginning with your costs or 'Cost Plus' pricing is simple and easy which is why so many people use this approach. However it doesn't take into account the money that you might be leaving on the table because the value greatly exceeds the cost of production. This approach was modelled by Dolan and Gourville in 2005 in their 'Value pricing thermometer', but has been in use since man started trading in antiquity.

'Value Based' pricing aims to place the product price as close as possible to the perceived value. It relies on understanding three things well. The costs of production, which are easy to measure and we are all used to, the perceived value, which will rely on pricing research if you want any degree of accuracy and the true economic value, which is harder again to quantify and relies as much on skill as research.

The ability to work with these three concepts and price accordingly is desirable skill. A marketer must raise the perceived value of a product as close to the true economic value as possible, encouraging customers to pay the highest price and maximising profit. Don't assume your customers perceive value in the same way as you do.

'Don't discount yourself, no matter what you are doing.'

Mark Zuckerberg, CEO and Founder, Facebook

Don't discount

Discounting is rife in the UK and dwarfs that in other European countries. It is one of the worst possible pricing strategies for a brand and has no place in pharmacy services. This is one area where even competing academics agree. You offer a premium healthcare product delivered by exceptionally well trained professionals in convenient and accessible surroundings. Recognise the value of that and don't discount. Communicate value instead.

Discounting can cause all sorts of problems that can affect the success of your pharmacy long term. It is the inverse of the unit price factor and has the same significant effect on profitability. Discounting to drive sales of a product can often be a false economy due to the impact on margin per unit. Sales may increase during the promotion but they will drop to normal levels as soon as it's stopped and at what cost? If you are considering doing this, calculate the total cost in £s of your promotion by multiplying the lost margin per unit by the expected increase in unit sales. Are you happy to give away that much profit for the sake of more sales? You may well have achieved the same sales over a longer period anyway.

Discounting causes customers to consider price above all else and commodifies the product. Commodities demand comparison based on price alone. Pharmacy services have a wide range of attributes that differentiate them from other providers and as such you risk commodifying if you discount them.

Pricing involves a lot of psychology. When you discount you are signalling that in some way the value of the product is lesser. This may cause customers to think the product is inferior and may cause pricing wars with competitors. Discounting also immediately damages brand loyalty. A higher price indicates quality which indicates brand strength and desirability.

If your basic pricing strategy is right you should not need to discount. Stick to your guns. Discounting is using tactics to fix strategy.

Really, don't discount

As a profession we haven't made the mistake of discounting. We have made an even bigger mistake. We have failed to charge at all for many of our most valued services.

Medicines advice and prescription collection and delivery to name two. We are suffering the consequences. That which is given freely is often perceived to have little or no value. To build our brand value as a profession we must avoid providing services for free or for lower remuneration than they are worth. We are competing inter-professionally for healthcare expenditure and must do all we can to communicate the value of our contribution if we want to win.

Free at the point of care

Unlike many other markets, what pharmacies get paid for delivering NHS services is fixed. We can't change it. Not quickly and without much effort and debate with our commissioners. With NHS services we can't use mainstream marketing techniques like lowering the price to attract more customers or increasing the price to signify better quality because customers don't pay at the point of care.

We need to find other ways to differentiate our NHS services by looking at the other Ps within the framework if we aim to secure market share from competitors whether they are within our profession or outside.

Price actions

1. Recognise the inherent quality in the professional services offered by pharmacies and aim to price your services based on the value they deliver.

2. Focus on your unit price and developing your product to allow you to set the price as close to the economic value as possible.

3. Don't discount.

Price notes

motion

[Place]

COMMUNICATION

Place

Place looks at the ways in which you get your product into your customers' hands.

Reaching your customers

Place is also known as distribution. While the vast majority of pharmacy services including retail sales and medicine supply are still provided from a physical pharmacy, a gradual expansion to include a remote, digital model is underway.

Many products are manufactured, sold to a wholesaler and then to a retailer. Others are sold directly to customers by manufacturers. Pharmacy involves a little of both. For the vast majority of physical products we sell or supply we are the last link in the chain before the customer. For some of those products we are the main permitted supplier by law, while others are open for sale by others. We are a supplier.

The less tangible products that we offer, such as advice, delivery, diagnostics, vaccinations etc might utilise manufactured products but we are the provider of those products to the customer. We are a provider.

In both cases we offer products directly to the customer. Our products are not resold by third parties on our behalf. We have a direct to customer distribution model which hasn't changed for decades. This is a strength we often underestimate. We are very close to our customers which gives us the opportunity to understand them better.

What is changing is the face to face method of delivery that is associated with a physical location and specific premises. The pharmacy. As society develops around us many of our customers' needs are being met in new ways utilising rapidly developing digital and logistical technologies. Customers may come to expect similar ways of accessing pharmacy services as they are using to access other services.

The global innovators in this area are smoothly integrating physical and digital experiences to produce a seamless customer journey. As customers we flip between physical and digital fairly fluently and we are coming to expect our preferred brands to adapt to that. Pharmacy has some unique challenges and should consider how best to meet this customer need.

This is a key battleground for the pharmacy profession in the coming years. One that we must take charge of ourselves if we are to thrive. The value we add to the supply function is plain for us to see every day. We need to continue to enhance that value, capture it, articulate it and communicate it while building new ways of delivering our services that utilise new technologies in ways that only we can deliver.

Do your market research to find out what your customers need and expect and begin from there. While the broad sweep of change may seem irresistible your customers are the key. Don't assume that they will automatically follow the global trends.

Omni-channel pharmacy

As customers come to expect an integrated approach to the delivery of pharmacy services (supply, retail and clinical), in line with innovations and developments in other areas of their lives, you need to consider how you can best meet their needs to remain competitive. This integrated approach, which combines physical and digital, local and remote, purchase channels is often called omni-channel. Omni literally means 'all' or 'in all ways'. There are, of course some services which can't be delivered remotely or digitally. However there are often aspects of these services, booking and after-care, for example which can.

The physical bricks and mortar delivery of services you will be familiar with, however you should apply the marketing process to ensure that you are using that space to its full potential. Review every aspect of the physical space you and your customers inhabit to identify ways in which you can adapt, adjust and if necessary and within budget, radically change it to meet current and anticipated future needs. The specific changes will be unique to your pharmacy. This might be as simple as a retail category review or as complex as a refit and automation project or even a relocation.

The smooth integration of service delivery from physical and digital channels is an important consideration and one that it isn't wise to delay. Even if after you have considered it you decide not to integrate the two, at least you have made a conscious decision. It is likely that you will decide, to some extent, to integrate which requires some thought. There really is a wide range of options and assessing where integration will add value for the customer is the key. You could choose to introduce automated dispensing in some form with equally automated customer alerts when medication is ready for collection. You might decide to install touch screens linking to your website allowing prescription requests online while in your pharmacy. You might decide to invest in touch screen retail displays minimising retail space and making more room for dispensing and service delivery. You might, but you should, only if it benefits the customer. Always keep that in mind and use it as a test during your thought processes.

The digital delivery of pharmacy services is opening up and offers significant opportunity for those who have the vision, insight, skills and courage to take it. There may well come a disruptive change in the delivery of pharmacy services as there has in many other areas. In the meantime, there are some simple steps you can take to make sure you deliver a good online experience for your customers and that there is a level of integration with your physical service delivery that you are happy with. Make sure your website is easy to find, up to date and communicates the right messages when users visit. You can decide whether prescription request functionality is useful. The same goes for service booking. Use your imagination about how you can deliver all or some aspects of any given service within legal, ethical and professional constraints. Do your customers really need an app? Does your social media channel deliver any value for your customers? Customers will add to their view of your brand at every touch point. Make sure that what you do, you do well.

Place actions

1. Harness the key advantage of the direct to consumer model, customer contact, to explore your customer needs in depth.

2. Explore as part of your market research, what mix of online and physical will work best for your customers over the coming months and years.

3. Develop your operational platform to deliver that mix and continue to monitor.

Place notes

People

>

BRA

[Promotion]

Pla

COMMUN

Promotion

Promotion looks at choosing the communication channels you use to send messages to your customers.

Integrated marketing communications

Promotion is the act of crafting your marketing messages to appeal to the target market and communicating where and when they will notice and respond to them. Developing an integrated schedule of marketing activity that includes message, time, frequency and communications channels enables you to implement, monitor and measure that activity.

All communications channels have strengths and weaknesses. They are just tools however. When choosing which to use to get your marketing messages across base your choice on which ones will do the job best. Do not base your choice on anything else, certainly not fashion or opinion. Focus on the ends before the means. Consider two key areas when selecting which communication channels to use.

Customer

Start with your customer. Think about where they spend their time whether that is physical or digital, how often they visit a particular place or platform, how long they spend there, why they go there and a whole host of other factors. If you think ahead when planning your market research you can gather a lot of this information before you need it. If your target market visits your pharmacy twice a week but spends little time on social media there will be a poor return on investing time in your social media content. Equally do you need to reach the people already visiting your pharmacy regularly or is it more useful to consider how to reach those that don't?

Brand position

Move onto your brand position. Think about the messages that you want to get across and whether the channel you are using supports that message. If you are promoting a weight management service there may be logic in advertising on fast food packaging rather than zero calorie drinks for example. There is an argument in both directions. It is easy to make mistakes here. Automated online advertising can appear next to content that runs in opposition to your own brand position. Be careful.

Media neutrality

An idea is independent of the media in which it is placed. No one communication channel is intrinsically better than another. This truth is known as media neutrality.

Professional marketers spend a lot of time comparing and debating the relative merits of a wide range of communications channels. TV, social, direct e-mail, website, outdoor advertising, sponsorship and more recently *programmatic* media, augmented reality, and virtual reality. The list goes on. People build up preferences for one or another communications channel often based on familiarity or new trends. Avoid this. It is not the right way to choose which communications channels to use.

Children receive liquid formulations because they often struggle to swallow tablets and capsules. Medicines that act in the intestines are given an enteric coating. Select the right communication channel to deliver your message to the people you want to reach, at the best time, in the best way, within your resources.

Think about where your customers can be reached, the message you want to get across and your marketing goals. Select the communication channels that will best achieve this. Don't just reach for the new, familiar or obvious.

Choose your channels

It can be daunting when you first start to build an integrated marketing communications plan. There are some very powerful global organisations, one begins with a G and another with an F, using their influence to compel you to use their particular communications channels. You know who they are. It may feel difficult to resist. Everyone else is doing it.

Resist. As a pharmacy look first at the channels that you have available to you at no or minimal cost and which are guaranteed to reach your target market and then broaden out your assessment of other channels. Remember, start with the ends in mind and consider whether each channel will or won't deliver the results you want.

In pharmacy

Exterior signage, window displays, interior signage, posters, leaflets, point of sale, in pharmacy events, promotional stands, product range, service range, environment, sales force.

Out of pharmacy

Leaflet drops, delivery driver leaflets, *stakeholder* leaflets / posters, partnerships, press releases, local events, local outreach services, stakeholder visits, sponsorship, sponsored events, your website, search, social media, advertisements.

This is by no means an exhaustive list but it will give you some food for thought when you start analysing which channels are right for your brand. Make a long list. Assess each on its merit. Narrow it down to a manageable selection that fits your budget. Better to do a great job with the channels you have at hand than a poor one with a huge range and fail to have an impact.

Traditional vs digital

From the early days of modern marketing, the range of ways in which brands have tried to reach their target markets has been growing. Since 1990 the digital revolution has resulted in an explosion of new communications channels all of which promise the earth. Remember that the owners of these channels are trying to sell you something not give you something and that you should analyse their usefulness in achieving your goals before you spend any money.

Digital channels are enticing. They are designed to be. The people selling them use the ideas in this book. People get very excited about these channels and many (not all) people use them in some way. While our children may be *digital natives* our parents are not and the latter group usually require more healthcare than the former. This situation will change, but gradually and it will be 35 to 40 years before retirees are digital natives.

Digital channels are often sold as a panacea for all, however they have their challenges. While they provide detailed metrics it is often hard to verify those metrics or even assign any real meaning to them. The people providing the data are the ones selling you the product. A clear conflict of interest. They have little incentive to tell you if their product isn't performing. Automated digital marketing risks your messages being displayed alongside messages from others that run in opposition to your own. There are of course some real opportunities when using digital communications channels and many people have done so very successfully. There may be a place for them in your marketing plan but only if you are basing their inclusion on their merits and you have compared their contribution with other channels. Uphold your media neutrality.

Do not even use the words 'traditional' or 'digital' and falsely put different communications channels into silos. Do not separate your marketing budget either. Your customers do not separate their lives in this way so your efforts will be wasted. More and more people are living in-between and within the physical and digital worlds and your goal must be reflecting that in your communications and how you deliver your pharmacy services across both dimensions.

'Marketing is simply when you let people know who you are and how you can help.'

Carrie Klassen, Writer, Artist, Creative

Channels, schedules, campaigns

When you are putting together your integrated marketing communications plan there are three broad steps to work through. Channel selection, scheduling and campaign development.

Channel selection

Start by selecting the communications channels that will deliver the best results and help you achieve your marketing goals. You will need to do this in the context of your budget and with a mind to the synergies you can achieve by using a range of channels rather than spending only on one.

Scheduling

Next build a simple schedule over time with each of your channels listed. This doesn't need to be complex or use special software, something like a spreadsheet is fine or even a pencil and paper to start with. You can build a communications plan with a baseline of activity that will act as a guide for frequency of activity for each channel, integration between channels and budget management.

Campaign development

Finally develop specific campaigns based on the messages that you want to communicate and populate your schedule with further detail about what content will be used, at what time and who will be tasked with implementing. This is when you can really work on synergies by timing communications across channels to have the maximum effect.

Make sure that you build in metrics with which to measure the effectiveness of your communications and to act as a guide for adjustment of your schedule over time. Many communications channels have built-in metrics and are a great place to start. You will learn whether your channel analysis was right and to what extent and you can adapt and try new approaches as you go. Don't forget to give your strategy and your plan, time to work before you start chopping and changing.

Promotion actions

1. Start with your customer then think about your brand position when selecting and analysing which communications channels to use. Do not select based on familiarity or new trends.

2. Utilise the free channels in your pharmacy first before you move onto expensive paid media.

3. Schedule and integrate your communications across multiple channels to deliver the best return on investment then execute with discipline.

Promotion notes

Case study | Step four

Product design

You begin making the interdependent set of tactical decisions to help you develop a stop smoking service that appeals to your target segments.

Product

You start by looking at your product. In this case the product is a stop smoking service.

The core benefits for your customers are reduced risk of various long term conditions, improved physical fitness and financial savings amongst others. You realise that while these seem obvious to you, they aren't to your customers and that you can highlight them more effectively during the customer journey to make sure every customer appreciates what is on offer. You take action and work on including references at each point in the customer journey.

The physical or actual products associated with the service are specified in the service level agreement which leaves you less room for manoeuvre in relation to the NHS commissioned service, however you realise that you can offer newer products as part of the private service that are not available on the NHS.

You take action and begin the accreditation process for supply of the new product. The pre-sales and after-sales aspects of your service are ripe for improvement and you decide to focus on these areas in both the NHS commissioned service and the private service. You take action and develop new ways of improving customer satisfaction including gathering case studies about successful quitters and organising annual quitter reunions.

Price

You accept that the remuneration you receive for the NHS commissioned service is fixed for now and you work with your local pharmaceutical committee to negotiate future remuneration contributing to and building on the existing evidence.

You calculate the costs involved with delivering the private service and consider the real value to a customer of successfully stopping quitting. You set an initial price for your private service based on the value it delivers for customers. You are working hard to deliver a premium service that meets customers' needs in ways that have not been available before. You are confident setting an aspirational price in the knowledge that you can always reduce the price if the market does not respond.

Place

Your pharmacy is located in the centre of town with good parking and is close to local amenities. Your opening hours are currently 9am to 6pm.

You have an accredited member of staff on duty Monday to Friday. You consider how to communicate this information to re-position your NHS commissioned service.

You want to reach out so you explore taking your stop smoking service to local community centres, religious centres, pubs and libraries.

You decide to open from 8am on Tuesdays and stay open until 8pm on Thursdays to provide specific stop smoking clinics as part of the private service and explore taking your service to local, member only gyms.

You decide to build an omni-channel service and develop automated messaging to deliver appointment reminders, provide encouragement and mark milestones for service users.

Promotion

You pull it all together and develop an integrated communications plan. You schedule the type, frequency and content of your marketing communications to get across how your services meet customer needs.

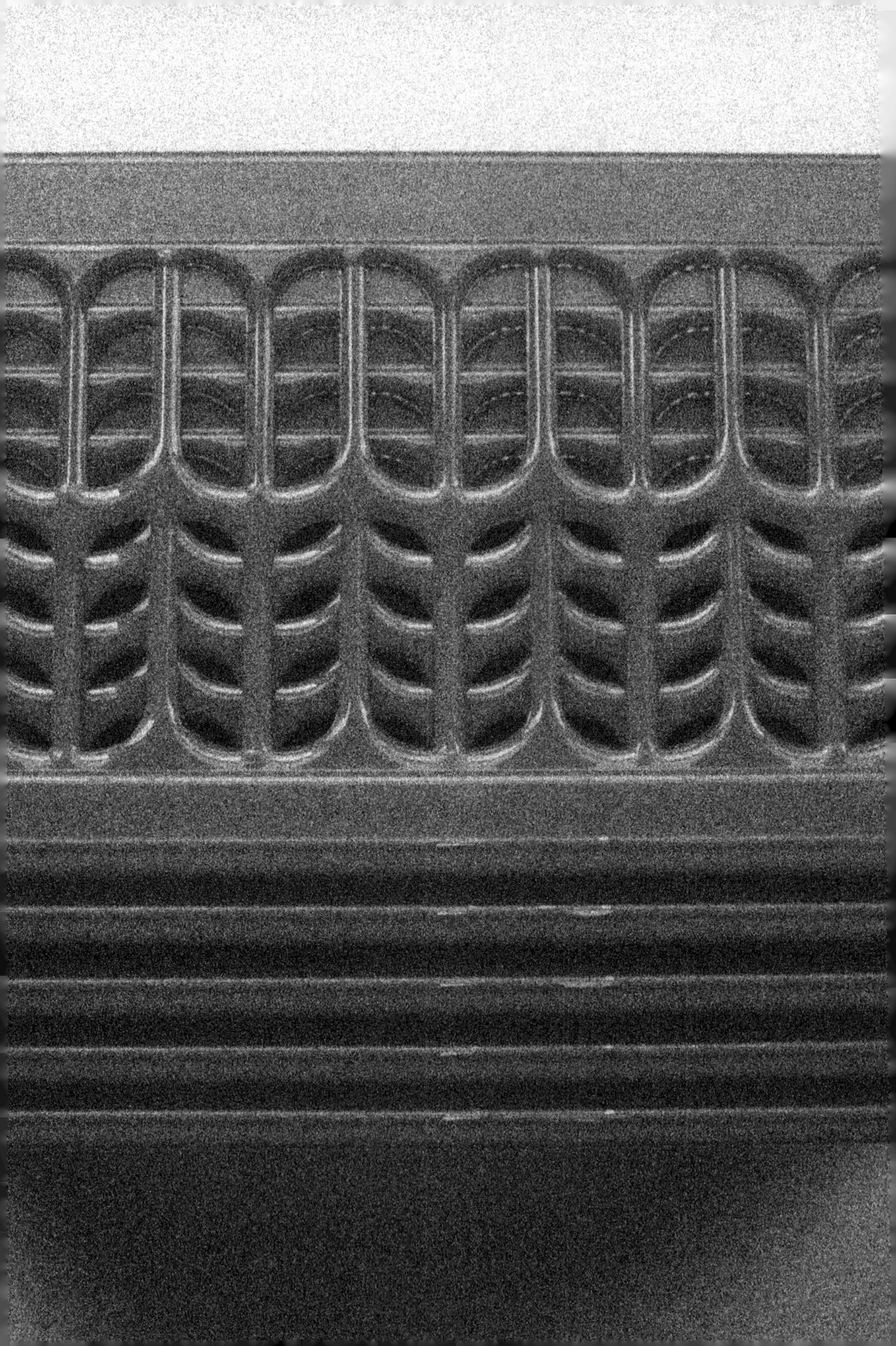

You realise that the choices are extensive and review all available communications channels. You calculate anticipated return on investment for each channel and make some initial decisions about which channels to use. You decide to use a range of in pharmacy channels and develop posters, leaflets, bag stuffers and a brief intervention script for your team.

You decide to use a range of out of pharmacy channels and after a launch event at your pharmacy you attend local community events. You arrange an interview on the local radio station, send a press release to your local paper and you invite the local MP to visit your pharmacy. You share information about your services online on your website and through your social media channels optimising all the way.

You organise your communications into specific campaigns focusing on each of your target segments sequentially. You adjust the messaging and creative in each campaign to appeal to the specific target segment you are targeting. You monitor response and adapt to amplify successful activity.

Step five

Step five looks at product delivery through the other three Ps of marketing. People, Process and Physical evidence which are important to consider. They were originally developed with the service industry in mind and fit pharmacy practice well.

Product delivery

+ People
+ Process
+ Physical evidence

The other 3 Ps of marketing

The other 3 Ps are focussed around service *tangibilisation*. That is the customer's experience of a service, many of which have little or no tangible basis that customers can sense. These last 3 Ps aim to change that with the aim of improving the likelihood that customers will use your pharmacy again. Important then. With the vast majority of pharmacies offering the same retail products, prescription medicines and services, a key way to offer something unique is to consider how you deliver these products. The 3 Ps help you to do that.

In the late 1970s it was becoming widely acknowledged by marketing people that the original 4 Ps model of marketing, while robust, required some expansion. In 1981 Booms and Bitner proposed the addition of three new Ps to the marketing model which coincided with rapid growth in the service sector in first world countries.

The original 4 Ps are a vital starting point when bringing your brand position to life and building an appealing offer for your target market. The 3 Ps add further scope to the framework and provide us with a way in which to manage and influence the customer's experience further.

Process

[People]

Promotion

People

People looks at harnessing your team to enhance customer satisfaction and build your brand.

People power

The people within your pharmacy team will have the biggest impact on your success. Everything they are, think, believe and do as a group will determine your future. Marketing is no exception and is in fact an area where their impact is sometimes underestimated if not overlooked.

Human nature dictates that customers struggle to separate a product from the person who provides it. We are all finely tuned to assess the people we come into contact with and how your pharmacy team behave will impact strongly on customer satisfaction. This is something you will already be aware of.

Customer satisfaction is the primary goal of your pharmacy, so your pharmacy team have significant control over your most important goal.

Work hard to ensure the right people, with the right attitude, right training and right personal skills are working together to optimise customer experience. Better still harness your team as a marketing tool and teach them about how they can help to build a successful pharmacy brand, day in day out.

You could involve them in the research and positioning process so that they understand what matters to your customers and what you are going to do to try and respond to that.

Personalised pharmacy

The practice of pharmacy is personal. We provide pharmaceutical care to people on an individual basis. It has always been that way. It is a real strength for pharmacy. However in many cases it is becoming harder. Increasing volumes and decreasing resources is putting personal pharmacy almost out of reach in some cases. Often the people delivering the care are not at fault and want to provide the same kind of care as they always have, but as systems develop to cope with change they inhibit that ability.

Don't let your processes and systems make it harder for your team to satisfy your customers. Focus on helping them understand the bigger picture about delivering customer satisfaction. Talk about it openly during team meetings as the ultimate aim for the organisation and provide coaching on an ongoing basis about how you see that working alongside Standard Operating Procedures to spell it out. Provide customer service and sales training for your team.

The flip side of the coin is managing your processes and systems to be supportive and subservient to customer satisfaction. Actively manage them. Empower your people to make decisions that override process, within relevant constraints, to deliver customer satisfaction and praise them when they do. By doing this you are building a culture that values your people and puts patient satisfaction at the core of your business. It will only work if you are committed to it as an individual, a team and an organisation.

People actions

1. Make sure that you operate your pharmacy with a market orientation and that in doing so you let your team focus on customers.

2. Involve your team in the marketing process and gain their input so they understand what you are all trying to achieve.

3. Coach your team around customer satisfaction and regularly measure it.

People notes

[Process]

People >

Process

Process looks at how the processes you employ influence customer satisfaction.

Customer satisfaction procedures

Pharmacy is built on processes and systems. Standard operating procedures (SOPs) govern the majority of what we do and we are expected to create and follow them. They are intended to ensure consistency of quality and a reliably high standard every time we complete a task. They are necessarily technically focused. I have written many but I have never read one that considers how the process will translate into customer experience.

If you are truly serious about marketing your pharmacy services you should consider developing an approach which takes a detailed look at the processes you employ not just from the technical, legal and regulatory perspective but also from that of customer satisfaction.

A set of SOPs as we know it span various interactions with customers and the activities that are necessary to support these. Why stop there? Develop a set of CSPs, Customer Satisfaction Procedures that start with the first customer point of contact which may be a website, a leaflet in your local surgery, a phone call, a social media post or even your pharmacy fascia and window display. They then follow the customer journey through individual services. Each CSP would consider how best to create the best experience possible within constraints.

Why leave it to chance? Why wonder whether your customer will return without doing everything you can do to influence that? Create a set of CSPs even if it is just for key services and use them to train your team on how to deliver the best possible service not just technical competence.

Process actions

1. Take one product at a time and ask your customers for feedback at each touchpoint.

2. Identity ways to adjust the current process to deliver better customer satisfaction.

3. Write a customer satisfaction procedure and repeat for all other products.

Process notes

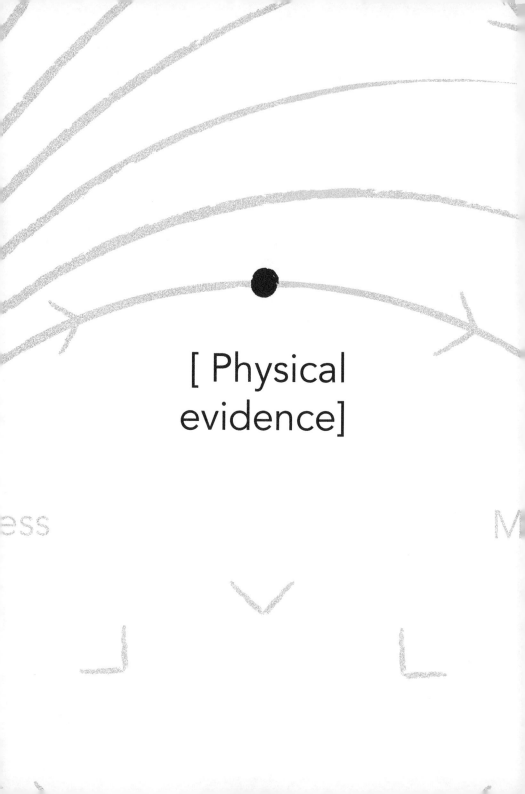

[Physical
evidence]

Physical evidence

Physical evidence looks at environment and the items and materials we leave with customers following service delivery.

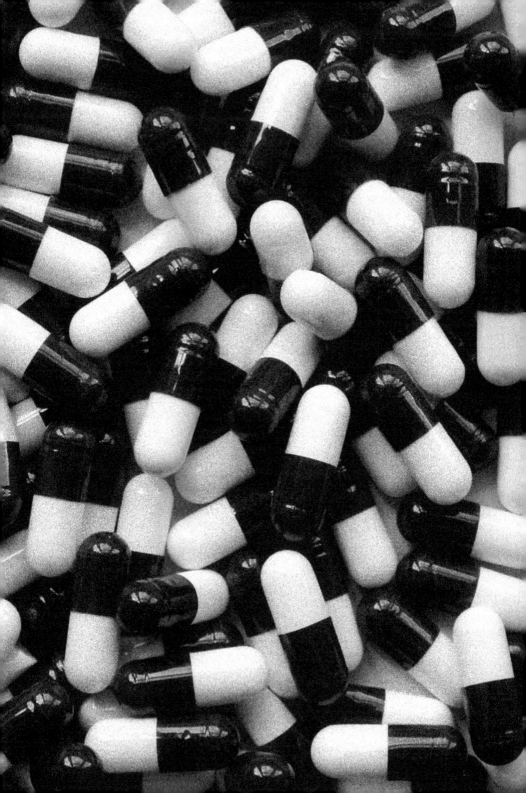

Prove yourself

Customers know what to expect when they come into your pharmacy to pick up a prescription or to purchase an OTC medicine. They've done that before. This may not be the case with a new service. If you provide some physical evidence of new products or services you will have a better chance of customers understanding how it can help them and therefore making a purchase.

Many of the services we have sought to develop as pharmacists in recent times have no tangible basis that customers can sense despite having a valuable health outcome. There is no obvious physical item they can take away from a blood pressure test or a vaccination if you discount the plaster. Providing high quality physical evidence can help. Consider putting together after care packs that not only provides a physical item as an outcome but can act as a reminder to return for future services. A branded tracker tool which supports patients seeking to manage their weight may be a daily reminder of how your pharmacy is helping them reach their health goals.

Your premises are critical. A clean, organised, well decorated pharmacy is reassuring as is a well designed modern website. If your premises don't reach customer expectations then why would your customers think differently about your services? Equally, if you are expecting people to trust you to deliver clinical healthcare services, let alone pay for them, they will need to be delivered within the right setting. Think about your consultation room design and whether it is clean, clear of stock and tidy. Balance the negative impression of a £1 discount bay and the profitability it delivers versus your ability to convince customers to pay £30 for a vaccine.

Gather testimonials from happy customers and share those. The credibility of customer testimonials cannot be overestimated.

Physical evidence actions

1. Consider what messages the physical environment in your pharmacy sends to your customers and make the necessary improvements.

2. Consider what messages your digital presence sends to your customers and make the necessary improvements as required.

3. Develop high quality materials to leave with your customers following service delivery.

Physical evidence notes

Case study | Step five

Product delivery

You realise how important your team are to customer satisfaction and that they are critical to successful marketing.

People

You take action. You have been involving your team in the marketing process from the start. You have been coaching them on the primary importance of customer satisfaction as the main goal of your pharmacy. You have arranged customer service and sales training to help them develop the skills they need to deliver the best possible experience for your customers and empower them to use their initiative to do so. They understand what can be done and what can't be done within professional, legal and ethical constraints.

You have developed ways of measuring customer satisfaction and how each of your team members are contributing to that. These measures are now a part of each individual's objectives and the key performance indicators for the pharmacy. Your team understand and have adopted a market orientation. It is embedded in your culture.

Process

You have taken a look at your standard operating procedures for your stop smoking services and updated them to include the improvements you have made to the NHS commissioned service and you have developed a new procedure for the private service. You have taken it a step further and developed them into customer satisfaction procedures including all of the important task orientated detail as well as customer service detail. You have involved your team in the development of the CSPs and they are engaged with delivering the highest levels of customer satisfaction.

Physical evidence

You have identified that your pharmacy environment, while reasonably good, could be better.

You take action. You have toned down the retail emphasis and enhanced the healthcare focus with new signage and by adjusting category layout. You have reviewed the entire pharmacy and removed any unnecessary fixtures, fittings, displays or promotional materials. You have replaced the retail display in the window with an educational, stop smoking display. You have created a health promotion zone. Your consultation room has been tidied and redecorated and you have set up all of the materials you need to deliver the service. You are considering updating the exterior signage and installing a second consultation room in six months based on response to your service development strategy.

You have reviewed your website and updated the areas that relate to the stop smoking service. You have carried out keyword research and have optimised the content to ensure the highest possible search engine ranking for stop smoking services in your local area. You refresh your social media presence with scheduled and well executed stop smoking related content.

You develop new materials to give to service users at each stage of their quitting journey, tailored to provide the right support and encourage them to return for their next appointment.

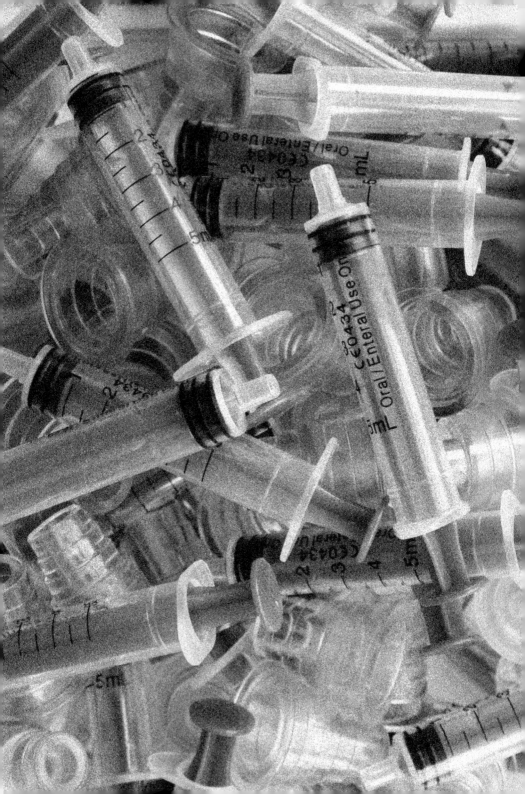

Combing the 7 Ps

Combining the 7 Ps looks at putting it all together and executing your strategic intent.

The best combination

The seven Ps of marketing must be considered in relation to each other. A pricing decision will have implications for every other P and vice versa. As you can now appreciate there are a wide range of ways to design the same pharmacy product depending on how you put together the seven Ps.

Hopefully you will understand that when working on your marketing you should start with your customer. Do the same when designing a new pharmacy product.

Carry out your market research to understand the customer needs and identify and characterise your target market segment whether based on function, personality or behaviour.

Determine how to position your service to meet your customers' needs and select a small number of attributes that you want people to associate with your product.

Consider each of the seven Ps and make a series of decisions about how best to design a service that meets customer needs at a profit that you are happy with.

Private vs NHS

Most companies constantly seek new ways to make their product stand out. To instil it with some magical property that other products just don't have and provide a reason for customers to buy. Note the incessant innovations in the shaving razor category or positioning fabric softeners as desirable, scent based, lifestyle must haves. This is a constant headache for marketers across the globe.

Private services are an open market. One that as a profession we have been touching on with success ranging from the sublime to painful. There are ways and means of designing unique services that can set you apart. Your imagination is the only limit. Think big and then make it fit within legal, ethical and professional frameworks.

Service design may seem to be something that only relates to private pharmacy services. While there is certainly more freedom without the restrictions of a Service Level Agreement don't be fooled into thinking this means you can't take action to market your NHS funded services.

I have never read a Service Level Agreement that includes a section about what you are not allowed to do. They are very descriptive about what must be done but seldom about how and never restrictive about doing a little bit extra to differentiate your service compared to other providers.

For NHS services some of the seven Ps won't be relevant and are wiped out by the SLA. Price for example is fixed. In some ways that simplifies things. You have to deliver the service to specification, within that pricing structure while making a profit. You can however look at how to add value for the customer through environment, location, service levels, process, and a whole host of other ways that will help you to recruit more customers and win market share. Many of the enhancements you put in place for one service will have an impact across all of your services including prescription services and even retail sales.

Think wider than your SLAs while delivering the best service for your commissioners and customers.

Metrics

Monitor response to your marketing activity against your SMART objectives and you will understand how effective your actions are. Marketing has long suffered from a seeming lack of solid metrics that prove or disprove the efficacy of any given action. In recent times the opposite has become a problem for some. Too much data. Building into your marketing plan how you intend to monitor success is critical. It helps you to move around the tactical cycle, test and adjust your actions. It helps you understand if and when to return to the strategic arc.

Aim to measure your marketing activity in three ways.

Firstly, use the analysis tools that are provided by the platforms you use to communicate with your target market. These are measures against criteria set by the platform provider mostly. They will provide you with some useful information that you can track over time and in response to changes to your activity. The people who sell these platforms recognise the need to provide evidence of their value. They succeed in that aim to varying degrees. Be cautious however because they have an interest in presenting the truth in a way that makes them look their best while at the same time providing an almost overwhelming amount of data that can confuse rather than illuminate.

Secondly, use the data you collect to define how well you are achieving the SMART objectives that you set yourself. This should be fairly simple as when you set the objective you defined how it would be measured. These are measures against criteria set by you, so they should be of high value.

Lastly, use your common sense. If you are achieving your overarching goal then you are doing something right. Keep doing it while using the above metrics to uncover in more detail how you can do it even better.

We are pharmacists. Accuracy is one of the things we do best. We are scientists. We measure and adjust. Measure your marketing.

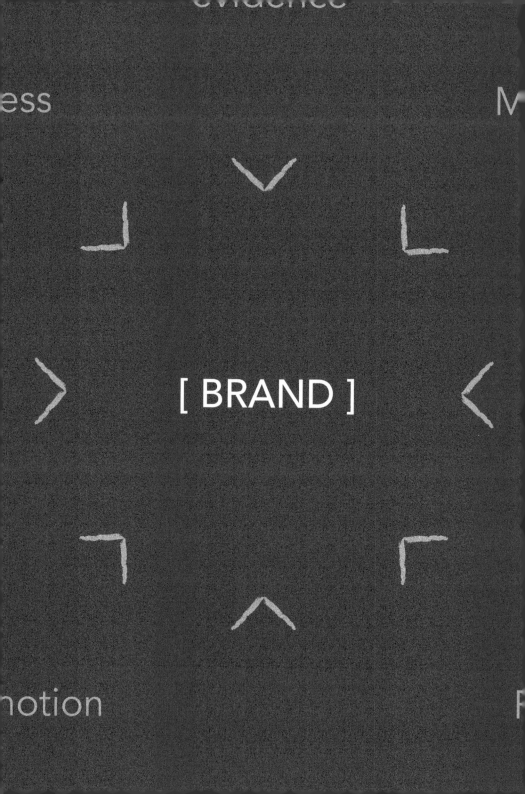

Brand

Brand looks at being recognised for the work you do and being thought of positively. Brand is the result of the marketing process and is what you are aiming to influence and manage during that process.

Brand value

The value of your brand is the meaning that differentiates it from the generic equivalent. You can literally take away the price of the generic equivalent from the price of the branded version to determine value of your brand, sometimes called brand equity.

This definition fits nicely into our profession. It's easy for us to understand. Pop into your local high street multiple pharmacy, perhaps the one with the blue colour palette, and compare the prices of their premium branded ibuprofen tablets with the generic Ibuprofen tablets. If you want to buy the leading brand with the silver packaging you will pay around seven times more per tablet. Seven times. We knew that already but it is still shocking. We know that the active ingredient is identical as is the pharmaceutical effect. Yet people are willing to pay seven times more than necessary to obtain the core benefit of the product. All of the work that the premium brand owners have done in positioning their product and expressing that through the seven Ps has enabled them to charge a huge premium which people are actually willing to pay. That is brand value. That is brand equity.

A commodity or generic equivalent involves two factors. Price and function. If the product delivers the function in the same way as competitors then price is the only factor people will consider when purchasing. Think of coal, milk, petrol or potatoes.

A brand has a third factor. Meaning. It is the defining characteristic of a brand. Anything that adds meaning is brand building. Anything that destroys meaning is brand destroying.

Brand value is affected by both the positive and negative associations that customers hold about the brand. It is the sum of the two. The calculation is carried out in the customer's mind. Your brand exists in the customer's mind and it is your job to try and influence it to be as positive as possible, to create meaning and to command a premium.

'A brand is what people say about you when you are not in the room.'

What is a brand?

Your brand exists in the mind of customers. In fact it is created there and is the result of the sum experience customers have of your products and pharmacy. You can't control peoples minds so how do you control their view of your brand? Well, you can't. The best you can hope to do is to influence their view positively and consistently.

Use the tools you have and that you are in control of. You have defined what you would like to stand for in your customers' minds when you established your brand position early on in the strategic process. You picked two or three key words, concepts or ideas you would like your customers to associate with you. That is your goal. The tools you have to try and create and maintain those associations are the seven Ps. How you choose to combine the seven Ps will affect your customers' experience which will determine their view of your brand and what they associate with you and your products.

Don't make the mistake of thinking that because you have just one pharmacy that you don't have a brand. You do. Every pharmacy company has a brand whether they recognise it, nurture it and protect it or whether they neglect it. Don't neglect your brand, because the more you manage and care for it, the more value it will add to your business. This value can insulate you against the hard times or add to the price you can command if your aim is to sell.

You could say that your brand is the synthesis of your positioning execution but that would be a little too technical and overdoing it a bit. When you are making decisions within the seven Ps framework keep in mind what you want to stand for and only do it If it helps to create a desirable association.

Fig 9. The brand equity equation

$$\boxed{\text{Brand}} - \boxed{\text{Commodity}} = \boxed{\text{Equity}}$$

Brand management

The effort involved in successfully creating positive brand associations in the minds of your customers is not inconsiderable. When you manage to get there you will want to stay there to make the hard work worthwhile and to reap the benefits. Staying there is called brand management. In its simplest form, brand management involves considering and looking after two areas. Brand image and brand awareness.

Your brand image is made up of the associations customers have gathered in their mind over time. They can be positive but they can also be negative. They can also change over time as they have new experiences and change their associations. This is one of the reasons to think of marketing as a long term ongoing process not a discreet activity. For example the pharmacy profession is seen as a reliable source of advice about medicines by the majority of the public. This is a long standing positive brand association.

Brand awareness is easy to understand but has a big impact. If you have created positive associations that position your brand as intended your challenge then becomes increasing awareness of your brand to the widest audience possible. If your target customer can recognise your brand and recall it when asked about your product category then you know you have good brand awareness. If asked where do you go to get your prescription medicines there are few in the country who would answer something other than pharmacy but would they answer your pharmacy?

Brand actions

1. Do not accept being seen as a commodity by customers. Use every possible opportunity to add meaning to your work and define your pharmacy as a brand.

2. Foster a practical awareness of that which builds your brand and that which damages your brand. Pursue the former and avoid the latter relentlessly.

3. Work hard to portray a brand image that represents your positioning and then consistently market your pharmacy to raise and maintain brand awareness.

Brand notes

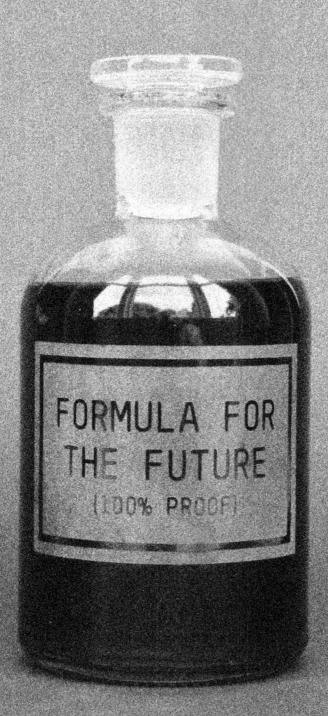

Pharmacy marketing

Pharmacy has meaning but we struggle to distil and communicate it. We add value to people's lives and we need to be better at communicating this value, both individually and collectively. Our future relies on learning to do this well. If we don't capture and get across why we are more than a logistics function, we will remain vulnerable to being replaced. The principles of design and marketing are universal so they apply to pharmacy just as easily as any other endeavour.

Our services are complex and highly regulated which often dominates our thoughts on how to deliver them. We need to think about how our services satisfy customer needs and what customers feel and think afterwards.

You are now armed with 5 steps and 64 ideas that are central to building a marketing strategy, helping you grow your pharmacy business and in doing so promote the profession at the same time. Work your way through each of the steps one by one. It will be a good use of your time. It will take longer than doing it ad hoc but it will be more effective and lasting.

Your strategy will need to adapt to changes in the environment around you. The pace of change will determine how often you need to review in depth, but it is a constant process of development and evolution that will result in the best strategic response to your environment. Look at your strategy regularly and review in full at least once a year.

Society's view of pharmacy and our place within it will be influenced by their experience of every individual pharmacy, pharmacy team, service and the work of our national bodies. We are in this together. We owe it to ourselves to develop the ability to manage our brand and to cooperate to take action over decades not months.

Take action. Market yourself, your pharmacy and our profession.

References and recommended reading

Here is a list of print and online sources that I have used during development of this book and of other useful references about marketing that I would recommend if you are inspired.

Bird, D. (2018) Drayton Bird Associates [Online], Available at: http://draytonbird.com/blog/ [Accessed 30 March 2018].

Dolan, R. and Gourville, J. (September 2005. Revised April 2009) Principles of Pricing. Brighton: Harvard Business School.

Doyle, P. and Stern, P. (2006) Marketing Management and Strategy, 4th Edition. Harlow: Pearson Education Limited.

Fahy, J. and Jobber, D. (2012) Foundations Of Marketing, 4th Edition. Maidenhead: McGraw-Hill Education.

Hoffman, B. (2018) The Ad Contrarian [Online], Available at: http://adcontrarian.blogspot.co.uk/?m=1 [Accessed 30 March 2018].

Lafley, A. and Martin, R. (2013) Playing To Win. Boston: Harvard Business School Publishing.

McCarthy, J (1960) Basic Marketing: A Managerial Approach Homewood: R.D.Irwin.

Office for National Statistics, (2017) UK Health Accounts: 2015 [Online], Available at: https://www.ons.gov.uk/peoplepopulationandcommunity/healthandsocialcare/healthcaresystem/bulletins/ukhealthaccounts/2015 [Accessed 30 March 2018].

Ritson, M. (2018) Marketing Week Focus Mark Ritson [Online], Available at: https://www.marketingweek.com/focus/mark-ritson/ [Accessed 30 March 2018].

Sharp, B. (2010) How Brands Grow. South Melbourne: Oxford University Press.

Stengel, J. (2011) Grow. New York: Crown Business.

Quote attribution

Here is a list of quotes with original sources where known.

P10 Ford, H. Original source unknown.

P12 Kotler, P. (2018) Kotler Marketing Group [Online], Available at: http://www.kotlermarketing.com/phil_questions.shtml [Accessed 30 March 2018].

P14 Druker, P. (2008) The Essential Druker: The Best of Sixty Years of Peter Drucker's Essential Writings on Management. New York: Harper Business.

P20 Ritson, M. (2018) Marketing Week [Online], Available at: https://www.marketingweek.com/2016/05/11/mark-ritson-beware-the-tactification-of-marketing/ [Accessed 30 March 2018].

P24 LeBoeuf, M. Original source unknown.

P60 Norman, D. Original source unknown.

P72 Schopenhauer, A. (2000) The World as Will and Representation: Volume 2. Mineola :Dover Publications Inc.

P82 Trout, J and Rivkin, S. (2008) Differentiate Or Die. New York: Crown Business. Hoboken:John Wiley And Sons.

P84 Sharp, B. (2010) How Brands Grow. South Melbourne: Oxford University Press.

P100 Dodaro, M. (2017) People don't care about your business. They care about their problems. Be the solution they are looking for. #SocialSelling [Twitter] 28th August. Available from: www.twitter.com [Accessed 30 March 2018].

P116 Kotler, P and Armstrong, G. (2010) Principles Of Marketing. London: Pearson Education.

P122 Godin, S. (2018) Seth Godin [Online], Available at: https://www.sethgodin.com [Accessed on 30 March 2018].

P132 Zuckerberg, M. Original source unknown.

P152 Klassen, C. (2018) Carrie Klassen [Online], Available at: http://www.carrieklassen.com [Accessed 30 March 2018]

P194 Bezos, J. Original source unknown.

Glossary

Customer: A person who invests in a product from a business.

Demographic: A word used to describe a particular section of a human population based on personal characteristics such as age, gender, ethnicity, geography etc. This relates to who they are.

Digital native: A person born or brought up during the age of digital technology who has not known a world prior to development of such technology.

Firmographic: A word used to describe a particular section of a business population based on organisational characteristics such as age, geography, scale etc. This relates to who they are.

Focus group: A group of people who are gathered to take part in a guided discussion about particular topic of interest to the organiser.

Heterogeneous: Diverse in content.

Homogeneous: Alike in content.

Marketing: Marketing is the science and art of exploring, creating and delivering value to satisfy the needs of a target market at a profit.

Product: A product is anything that can be offered to a market for attention, acquisition, use or consumption.

Positioning: The process of selecting and communicating a set of attributes for which the brand would like to be known in the mind of customers.

Programmatic media: The algorithmic sale, purchase and implementation of digital advertising in real time.

Prospect: A person who is seen as a potential customer for a product. I haven't confused the issue in the main text by using this word. When you are marketing you may be trying to reach your customers, your prospects or both.

Psychographic: A word used to describe a particular section of a human population based on psychological characteristics such as attitudes, beliefs and behaviours etc. This relates to what they think and do.

Qualitative: Measuring based on quality not quantity.

Quantitative: Measuring based on quantity not quality.

Salience: The quality of being particularly noticeable or important.

Segment portrait: A description of a group of people who are alike in their characteristics and are a potential target market for a product.

Stakeholder: A person with an interest in a particular enterprise.

Strategy: A set of decisions designed to guide tactical actions in the pursuit of a long term goal.

Tactics: A set of actions designed to execute strategic decisions in the pursuit of a specific goal.

Tangibilisation: The conversion of something intangible into a tangible form.

Touch points: A point of contact or interaction, especially between a business and its customers.

The author

I remember it well. It was late September 1995. I was in the front room of my parents' house in Crosby, Merseyside. It was raining outside. My dad was sharing his wisdom about life and advising me about which university courses to apply for. I wanted to be a marine biologist but the family consensus was that a vocational course that would result in guaranteed income was better. I deferred to the consensus. However, I didn't fancy looking at old men's bunions so I declined medicine (little did I know about scrotal trusses at that tender age). That was how I became a pharmacist and I'm glad I did.

I am now 40 years old. I get bored easily and I'm addicted to learning new things so here is a list of the things I have spent my time doing since summer 2000 when I qualified as a pharmacist.

Locum pharmacist in community pharmacy and hospital. Pharmacy manager at Lloyds Pharmacy. Teacher practitioner at Lloyds Pharmacy and Bradford University. Member of the steering group establishing the UCLan School Of Pharmacy. District Manager and Area Manager at Lloyds Pharmacy. Post Graduate Certificate in Management at Northampton University. Committee member at Central Lancashire LPC. Community Pharmacy Advisor and Prescribing Support Pharmacist at Central Lancashire PCT. Operations Manager, Superintendent Pharmacist, Operations and Marketing Director at the multi-award winning Medicx Pharmacy. Chemist and Druggist Clinical Service of the Year 2011, first place. HSJ Managing Long Term Conditions Award 2011, finalist. Chemist and Druggist Platinum Design Awards 2010 and 2012, third then second place. BPSA conference presenter. Pharmacy transition board member at NHS Lancashire. Member of the NPA Innovation Board. Blogger at Chemist and Druggist.

As you can see I really do not like standing still.

In 2013 I decided I wanted a change and over two years, conducted the first global research into the brand of pharmacy as part of a Masters in Graphic Design at UCLan. This set me off on a course of trying to make a difference to pharmacy in my own unique way.

I set up DOSE Design and Marketing Ltd, a specialist pharmacy design and marketing agency in 2015 and so far have helped over 30 clients promote their pharmacy organisations more effectively. I've completed Advanced Wordpress training with Mike Little, co-founder of Wordpress and studied Marketing under Professor Mark Ritson. I'm currently studying for a Diploma in Photography.

I set up DOSE Publishing Ltd in 2016 and you are reading the first work to come out of that! These things take time.

There is more.

Chemist and Druggist Awards Business Initiative Of The Year 2016, finalist. Fellow of the Royal Pharmaceutical Society 2016. Chemist and Druggist Awards Judge 2016, 2017 and 2018. Pharmacy Show speaker (Pharmacy Branding and Pharmacy Marketing). Pharmacy Business Awards Conference speaker (Pharmacy Marketing). Pharmacy Forward speaker (Pharmacy Marketing).

Pharmacy has made all of this possible and offers endless opportunities only restricted by your imagination.

Call to action!

I genuinely hope that you feel inspired. Marketing is often one of the missing pieces of the jigsaw when operating a pharmacy. It needn't be. If you would like some help with working through the process in more detail, developing your branding and creating marketing campaigns that work, DOSE Design and Marketing can help. Get in touch and we'll be happy to get started.

Web: www.dosedesign.uk
E-mail: gavin@dosedesign.uk
Twitter: GavinAtDOSE
LinkedIn: DOSE Design and Marketing

DOSE Design and Marketing

It was raining. It was dismal. It was deepest, darkest London in 2013. Turning a corner there was a kebab shop. Oh hang on, it was actually a pharmacy. It just looked like a kebab shop. This was not good enough.

A Masters in Graphic Design (researching the brand of pharmacy) later and we set up our company to help pharmacy people promote their organisations better. It's a grass roots thing. Start working with real people and gradually make a difference to how pharmacy is perceived by the rest of the world. At the last count we've worked with over 30 organisations and we are still striving to make a difference. We are the design and marketing experts in pharmacy and work with pharmacy contractors and those selling into pharmacy every day.

We help pioneering leaders to develop effective marketing strategies.

We help ambitious organisations to build a brand that means something to their audience.

We help dynamic teams to plan and execute marketing campaigns that work.

Join us.

Thanks

I would like to thank Victoria Birchall, Steve Mosley and Steve Jeffers who took on the challenge of being first readers amongst other things and provided great feedback and encouragement. I'd like to thank George Birchall who went through the penultimate draft with a fine tooth comb for spelling, grammar and punctuation.